DISCOVERING
WHALES
OF THE EAST COAST

BY STEPHEN MULLANE

About the Author: Stephen Mullane has studied whales off the coast of Maine for the greater part of his adult life. Graduating from the College of the Atlantic in 1981, he pursued his interest in cetacean life by joining the Whale Watch program of Allied Whale. Stationed for four years on Mount Desert Rock, off the coast of Maine, he conducted marine mammal, seabird, and migratory bird studies. His photographs have been featured in books and magazines and he has contributed to the North Atlantic right whale, the finback whale, and the humpback whale research catalogs. He now divides his time between his two passions: whale-watching in the Gulf of Maine and boatbuilding amongst the famous boatbuilders of "downeast" Maine.

Front Cover: Humpback whale breach. These baleen whales always delight in their acrobatics. **Photo by François Gohier**

Left: A beluga appears as an angel out of the darkness. **Photo by Flip Nicklin / Minden Pictures**

Above left: The sight of a northern right whale is thrilling, as they are some of the rarest animals on the planet. The callosities seen on their odd-shaped heads are covered by amphipod parasites. **Photo by Hiroya Minakuchi / Seapics.com**

Above right: A humpback whale surfaces with a mouthful. The expanded folds or "rorqual grooves" are clearly visible. These grooves allow the rorqual whales to engulf large amounts of water which is then filtered through the baleen. **Photo by Beverly Agler**

Designed and published by Elan Publishing, Inc. 95 Deerwood Drive, Suite A. Charlottesville, VA 22911. For distribution and ordering information please call: 1-800-284-6539. Join us online at www.Elanpublishing.com. Discovering Whales of The East Coast © 2004 by Elan Publishing, Inc. All rights reserved. No part of this publication may be reproduced, stored in any retrieval system, or transmitted in any forms or by any means, without the written permission of the publisher.
Illustrations © Pieter Arend Folkens. All maps © Equator Graphics/IMA.
Library of Congress Catalog Number: 2001087820   ISBN number: 0-9672957-1-8
Proudly designed and produced in the United States of America. Printed in China.

INTRODUCTION

There are few experiences as full of excitement, joy, and mystery as seeing a whale or a dolphin for the first time. Whales and dolphins attract our attention because of their beauty, their often amazing size, and because of the mysterious world they inhabit. We, as humans, remain in awe when faced with whales and dolphins and our admiration for them has only deepened with the increased knowledge made available to us by new scientific research. Whether it is because of the thrill of not knowing where and when they will appear at the surface, the wildness about them, or just the glow of sunlight shimmering off their smooth skin, a meeting with whales and dolphins is exciting and memorable.

Humans and whales have interacted for thousands of years. Since the lives of whales were shrouded in mystery, stories and legends were born, and whales became part of the folklore of many societies around the world. Mixed with the riddle of their lives, their beauty, their strength, and even their intelligence, whales became the inspiration for art, music, songs, and literature. From primitive rock carvings found the world over, to frescoes, sculptures, painted vases, and mosaics fashioned by the classical Greeks and Romans, to today's more realistic representations, the beauty and gentleness of dolphins and great whales have inspired our creativity and compassion. Larger whales have also taken the role of sea monsters in many of our ancient histories. The whales' often impressive size made them powerful and potentially fearsome creatures, especially when coupled with human ignorance.

Whales have played an important role in the lives of people throughout the world as a

The sight of a dolphin gliding at the surface is always thrilling. Here a common dolphin graces the water in the area of the "Gully" just off Nova Scotia in the North Atlantic. Dolphins have never ceased to amaze humans throughout history. They were part of Greek mythology and were considered sacred. The origin of the word dolphin comes from the Greek "delphys," a word meaning womb, source of life. The Greek philosopher Aristotle (384-322 B.C) had already described in his Historia Animalium, species such as the killer whales, dolphins, sperm whales, and right whales, and had described them correctly as mammals.
Photo by Robin W. Baird / Seapics

Left: A humpback whale diving at sunset in the Gulf of Maine, just off Mount Desert Island and Acadia National Park, Maine.
Photo by Stephen Mullane

Right: The powerful breach of a humpback whale. The sound of a breach may carry for several miles across the water and further below the surface. Breaching may be a form of communication, a social display, a way of ridding the body of skin parasites, or simply an act of exuberance. Whatever the reason, they are a delight to witness and are awe inspiring.
Photo by François Gohier

source of food and commerce. Primitive societies initially took advantage of the sizeable bounty available when they happened upon beached animals. Later, hunting techniques were developed using canoes and kayaks, first near shore then progressively farther out at sea. As human societies evolved and the desire for food and whale products increased, hunting techniques advanced, as well as the technology involved in the hunt. Hand-propelled harpoons and lances were replaced by cannon-fired harpoons with exploding heads. The result for many species was the depletion of populations to alarming levels.

In the last thirty years, attitudes have changed in response to the increased awareness about the plight of whales and the deteriorating health of the world's oceans. Whales became the central focus for international efforts to preserve species and habitats. Research and preservation, as well as education through various media, museums, aquariums, and whale-watching trips, are now being focused in a world which continues to pollute its oceans, deplete its resources, and threaten the very existence of whales.

In this book we will explore the lives of whales and dolphins by introducing the species more commonly found along the East Coast of North America; from Florida to the Canadian Maritimes. Near this coast resides a wonderful diversity of whales, including one of the smallest, the largest, the deepest-diving, and the rarest. This region offers the seasoned, or first time whale-watcher the potential for amazing sights and life experiences.

CETACEANS

Just like humans, whales, dolphins, and porpoises are mammals. They are warm-blooded, breathe air, give birth to live young, and have mammary glands for nursing. A few even have some hair as adults, but most lose what hair they have during embryonic development.

Whales, dolphins, and porpoises are classified as members of the order Cetacea, within the class Mammalia, which includes all mammals from bats to elephants. Mammals, birds, reptiles, amphibians, and fish, as well as their extinct ancestors, are members of a large Subphylum called Vertebrata, or animals with a backbone. Members of the order Cetacea, called cetaceans, are divided into two groups, or suborders. The toothed whales, or Odontoceti, which all have teeth; and baleen whales, or Mysticeti, which have a series of keratinous plates, or baleen, attached to their upper jaw instead of teeth.

Whales and dolphins are often referred to as marine mammals, a term that includes dugongs and manatees, seals, walruses, sea lions, sea otters, and even polar bears. Only the manatees, dugongs, and the whales remain in the water for their entire lives. This means everything they do: breathing, feeding, mating, giving birth, nursing young, playing, sleeping, communicating, and migrating all occur while in the water. Much of their morphology, physiology, and behavior has evolved to protect against, and take advantage of, a life in water.

The study of fossil records has shown that cetaceans are descendants of terrestrial ancestors which are also related to present-day ungulates such as camels, pigs, deer, and hippos. Many shared morphological characteristics and genetic data are presently supporting the the-

A Finback whale rushes after bait at the surface. The finback is one of the fastest baleen whales. It can reach speeds of up to 20 to 25 miles per hour (32 to 40 km/h) in bursts. This speed is used primarily to overtake fast moving prey.
Photo by Stephen Mullane

Cetaceans (from the Greek ketos: sea monster/ whale and the Latin cetus: large sea animal)

Classification:
Kingdom: Animalia
Phylum: Chordata
Subphylum: Vertebrata (with backbone)
Class: Mammalia
Order: Cetacea (whales & dolphins)
Suborders:

Odontoceti   Mysticeti
(toothed whales)   (baleen whales)

Left: A mother and calf blue whale. The largest creature ever known in the animal kingdom, the blue whale reaches lengths of 100 feet (30.4 m) and 180 tons (163,000 kg). Already 21 feet (7 m) at birth, a blue whale calf will gain 150 pounds (68 kg) and grow at an incredible 1½ inches (3.8 cm) a day during the first six months of life. Found in all oceans of the world, the blue whale was hunted to the brink of extinction during the 20th century. A few populations remain, and too, the hope that they will survive.
Photo by Phillip Colla / Seapics

Right: The beloved bottlenose dolphin. Other than a remarkable diversity of adaptations to a whole range of environments across the globe, what all toothed whales have in common are teeth, in sharp contrast with the development of whalebone, or baleen, used by the baleen whales. Toothed whales hunt and target individual prey species, whereas baleen whales have evolved to feed on large amounts of prey filtered from the water.
Photo by Mark Jones / Minden Pictures

ory that cetaceans are closely related to hippos. During the Eocene Epoch, between 55 and 34 million years ago, the earliest form of cetaceans evolved from terrestrial ungulates and within a few million years were adapted to a fully aquatic life. The typical archeoceti, or archaic whales, had a pointed snout with many teeth, a squat body form, widely spaced fore and hind limbs, and odd-numbered toes ending with hooves. Those on the ancestral line to modern cetaceans trace the reduction in the size and use of the hind limbs, the development of paddle-like forelimbs, the transition between quadrupedal paddling to vertically oscillating tail flukes, and a host of other adaptations. By the beginning of the Oligocene, around 34 million years ago, the first baleen and toothed whales had appeared.

As some continents collided into one another and others moved farther apart, vast changes in the oceanographic and atmospheric conditions occurred. Changes in water currents and temperatures had a direct impact on the availability, quantity, and distribution of food. This impacted cetacean evolution, affecting how new species took advantage of the available food sources. Some evolved many baleen plates used to filter feed abundant small prey and became what we now know as the mysticetes. Others developed methods of echolocation used to hunt down larger individual prey; we know them as odontocetes or toothed whales.

The Miocene Epoch, from 23 to 5 million years ago, saw a great diversification in both baleen and toothed whales. Each suborder continued its evolution, and by the late Pliocene, about 1.8 million years ago, some modern species of cetaceans were already roaming the earth's oceans.

The physical characteristics of water and changes in habitats have shaped the evolution of cetaceans from the earliest archaeocetes to modern species.

Water conducts heat away from a warm body nearly 25 times faster than air. This rapid heat loss, especially in the seasonally frigid waters off the East Coast, requires both good body insulation and an abundant food source to supply the necessary heat energy to stay warm.

Whales have developed a layer of insulating fat just below the skin known as blubber. The blubber layer of energetic dolphins is about an inch thick, while the baleen whales may have a layer that is up to two feet thick! This layer of fat helps maintain a constant body temperature at around 98.6° Fahrenheit (37°Celsius), and also provides an important food reserve during lean times. Migratory

whales, especially females nursing calves, rely heavily on the blubber while they are in less productive tropical waters.

Some of the whales found along the East Coast spend a portion of each year in cold water, some venturing to the edge of the arctic pack ice. Cold water currents flow south from the coast of Labrador around Nova Scotia into the Gulf of Maine. This flow, or Labrador Current, as it is called, turns the northern and eastern portions of the Gulf of Maine into an extension of the Arctic Ocean. Many of the whales, seabirds, seals, and fish commonly found farther north are also found here. Even whales remaining in warmer surface waters may, like the sperm whale, feed thousands of feet below the surface where heavier cold water flows in a thick layer over the bottom.

Water is a rather viscous fluid, creating drag on any object trying to move through it. Animals in aquatic environments need to reduce the amount of drag and the energy

Above: Close-up view of a baby sperm whale eye. Who is watching whom? Peering into the eye of a whale can be among the most mysterious experiences of all. What does this eye see? What does the whale understand? We can examine the make-up of the eye, dissect its parts and guess at how well or poorly it sees in and out of the water, but we know nothing about how the whale interprets what it *sees, and little about the world that it experiences each day in the watery depths. Just imagine what a sperm whale sees three thousand feet below the surface while giant, luminescent squids shoot by in the dark abyss. Therein lies the mystery of every whale. Will we ever know?*
Photo by Doug Perrine / Seapics

ODONTOCETES AND MYSTICETES

All whales and dolphins are divided into two suborders of the Cetacean family: The toothed whales, or Odontocetes, which have teeth; and the baleen whales or Mysticetes which, instead of teeth, have baleen (some baleen whales will have embryonic vestiges of teeth). There are more species of toothed whales. Of the 80 plus species of identified whales only 12 are baleen whales. While there is some overlap in size, most baleen whales are longer and heavier than the largest of toothed whales. (see text)

The Mysticeti whales have many fibrous keratin plates which grow down from the roof of the mouth. This material forms a fine sieve on the inside and is used to catch prey. Baleen whales have two blowholes protected by a prominent "splashguard." The baleen whales' skull bones are symmetrical. The upper jaw and supporting skull bones are arched to support the baleen. In right and bowhead whales the upper jaw is arched markedly to support their very long baleen plates. The lower jaws are separated for almost their entire length and broadly arched from side to side. This provides a wide area for the large amount of water and prey to enter the mouth during feeding.

The odontocetes have true teeth, and a single blowhole without a "splashguard." The lower jaws in many species, especially members of the dolphin family, are fused for a considerable length. Toothed whales have highly developed echolocation apparatus including many anatomical refinements in the skull and lower jaw to assist in the production of sounds and the reception of reflected echoes. Many have distinctive beaks, smooth skin and dorsal fins.

Cetacean skeletons show particular adaptations to the life at sea. The cervical vertebrae

in most species are fused to strengthen and steady the head against the powerful up-and-down movement of the body. Most species lack skeletal hindlimbs, except for some vestigial bones in some larger species. Compared to land mammals, Cetacean bones are a lot lighter as buoyancy helps them carry their weight in water.

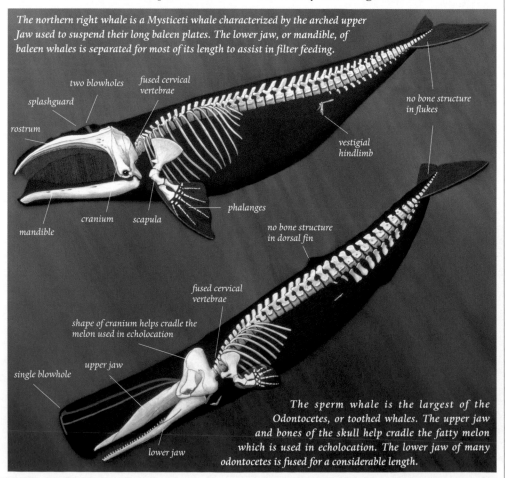

The northern right whale is a Mysticeti whale characterized by the arched upper Jaw used to suspend their long baleen plates. The lower jaw, or mandible, of baleen whales is separated for most of its length to assist in filter feeding.

two blowholes
splashguard
fused cervical vertebrae
rostrum
no bone structure in flukes
vestigial hindlimb
mandible
cranium
scapula
phalanges
fused cervical vertebrae
no bone structure in dorsal fin
shape of cranium helps cradle the melon used in echolocation
upper jaw
single blowhole
lower jaw

The sperm whale is the largest of the Odontocetes, or toothed whales. The upper jaw and bones of the skull help cradle the fatty melon which is used in echolocation. The lower jaw of many odontocetes is fused for a considerable length.

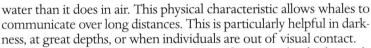

whales have lost their hair, some still have a few follicles on the head and snout. There are many sensory nerves at the base of these hairs, suggesting that they may be useful in sensing water currents or the presence of prey.

Of all the adaptations to life in water, the most impressive and sophisticated center on the use of sound in communication and echolocation. Sound travels four times faster and much farther in water than it does in air. This physical characteristic allows whales to communicate over long distances. This is particularly helpful in darkness, at great depths, or when individuals are out of visual contact.

Many species of whales have a variety of patterned pulsed sounds that may be used to communicate identity, location, and activity. While researchers have not been able to associate particular sounds with specific behaviors, they have noted changes in the number and intensity of calls with certain activities. Some whales call excitedly and frequently when meeting other groups they have not been in contact with for several hours or days and some call constantly while traveling, presumably to stay in contact with one another.

required to overcome it. This is accomplished by streamlining the body. Over the course of evolution whales have undergone many changes that have improved their ability to move through water more efficiently, and thus expend less energy.

The early ancestors of whales were four-legged relatives to present day ungulates, such as pigs and hippos. Through evolution whales have lost their hind limbs, and the forelimbs have developed into streamlined, paddle-like flippers. External sexual organs have moved within the body and are extruded through slits as needed; external ears have disappeared as well. Further streamlining is accomplished by the blubber layer below the skin. The blubber layer is not uniform in thickness, it is thicker posterior to the head and becomes thinner toward the tail. The resulting tapered shape reduces drag even more.

Hunting swift-moving prey required powerful locomotion. Whales solved this through a broadened tail that is pumped up and down rather than side-to-side as fish do. In all but the sperm whale, the nares, or external breathing orifices, migrated from the front of the head to the top. Blowholes, a single one for the toothed whales and two in baleen whales, are situated on top of the head to allow the whales to move more efficiently through the water as they breathe. This may also help their survival as it reduces the amount of time spent at the surface where whales are vulnerable to predators like killer whales and some sharks.

The insulative value of fur is lost when diving to great depths, and hair is an additional source of drag. Although

Above left: A humpback surfacing, clearly showing the distinct pair of blowholes common to baleen whales. The prominent ridge forward of the blowholes is known as the "splashguard," as it diverts water away from the orifices during respiration.
Photo by Stephen Mullane

Above right: A single blowhole is visible on this speedy white-sided dolphin exhaling at the surface. Breathing through nares at the top of the head allows cetaceans to move through water more efficiently, and reduces the time required at the surface where they are vulnerable to predators.
Photo by Stephen Mullane

Right: This view shows the streamlined bodies of the sei whales, here a mother and calf photographed in the North Atlantic. Streamlining is an essential adaptation for a life in water. Pointed heads, smooth skin with little or no hair, paddle-shaped flippers, and the loss of hind limbs are a few of the many streamlining adaptations that have occurred through evolutionary change. Diminishing drag reduces the amount of energy needed for locomotion.
Photo by Doug Perrine / Seapics

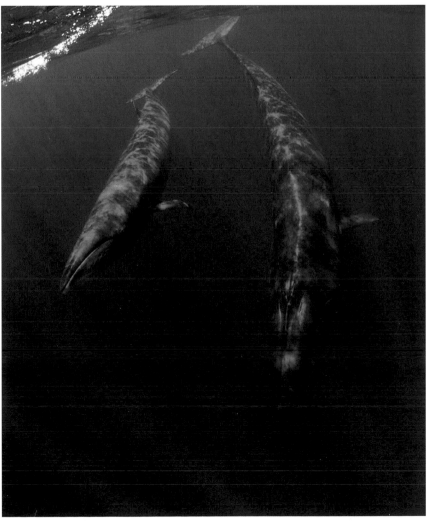

In some species, communication may aid in coordinating hunting activities, travel, rest, and alerting others to food, predators, and

possibly even expressing a wide range of emotions.

Many species of toothed whales have complex social structures, with communication through sound playing a major role. Toothed whales also produce a wide range of sounds used in echolocation. By adjusting the frequency of pulsed sounds, toothed whales are able to use echolocation to "see" objects over a wide range of distances and environments, including total darkness or buried in sand. Echolocation is also used in navigation (See sidebar page 14).

Baleen whales produce low frequency pulsed sounds that may be used in echolocation, to locate large objects at great distances, such as sea mounts, coastlines, and islands, and also for communication. Baleen whales also produce extremely powerful low frequency sounds below the range of human hearing. If produced under the right conditions, in layers of cold water deep below the surface, these sounds have the power to travel thousands of miles. It is quite possible that these whales are aware of other members of their species and communicate over these extraordinary distances.

In order to dive deeply and remain below the surface for long periods, cetaceans have developed a number of adaptations to cope with pressure and limited oxygen reserves. All diving mammals store oxy-

gen in their lungs, blood, and muscles. Cetaceans have a high volume of blood and a higher number of oxygen-carrying red blood cells per unit volume of blood than terrestrial animals. This means there are many more cells available to transport oxygen in the lungs to the muscles and other organs of the body. The muscles are rich in myoglobin, a protein that holds oxygen atoms until they are needed by the muscles. The lungs of whales are highly efficient in exchanging oxygen for waste carbon dioxide in the blood. When

humans breathe, only 26 percent of the oxygen taken into the lungs is absorbed by the blood, whereas in whales almost 80 percent is absorbed.

When whales dive they experience tremendous changes in pressure. This pressure ordinarily would force nitrogen gas in the lungs to be absorbed by the bloodstream. During the whale's return to the surface the nitrogen would come out of solution as bubbles in the bloodstream, disrupting normal flow and possibly killing the animal. Whales avoid this problem, commonly referred to as "the bends," by storing air in non-absorbing bronchial passageways when the lungs collapse under pressure.

Whales breathe air but feed and travel underwater. To do so efficiently they have developed great diving capabilities. With the advent of recent technologies, such as tagging devices using radio transmitters, satellites, and special underwater microphones, scientists have been able to study aspects of the underwater world of whales and their diving abilities. Sperm whales, for exam-

Above left: A pair of juvenile Atlantic spotted dolphins move in unison in a beautiful underwater ballet. The sense of touch is well-developed in cetaceans, especially in dolphins, which are often observed rubbing and stroking one another. Sensitive and sensual physical contact are important components of dolphin interaction.
Photo by Brandon D. Cole

Above: A humpback whale diving into the blue depths. Male humpback whales sing extraordinary songs while suspended head down in the water at their winter breeding grounds. Thought to be a sexual display, the songs are among the most haunting and beautiful sounds in nature.
Photo by Flip Nicklin / Minden Pictures

Left: Unlike the moans, groans, and whistles of humpback whale songs, sperm whales communicate through a wide variety of clicks arranged in subtle patterns known as "codas." What each coda means is unknown, but they are most commonly used as sperm whales gather at the surface between hunting dives, suggesting the importance of sound communication among these social whales.
Photo by Brandon D. Cole

ple, usually dive at depths of 900 to 2,000 feet (300-600 m) but individual dives have been recorded to depths of up to 9,850 feet or 3,000 meters and lasting as long as 2 hours and 18 minutes! Other large whales, such as the humpback, dive regularly for about 3 to 9 minutes but can remain submerged for up to 40 minutes. Finback whales usually dive for about 5 to 15 minutes and reach depths of up to 750 feet or 230 meters. Dolphins dive for shorter periods of time, usually less than 15 minutes for the bottlenose dolphin, and only 2 to 6 minutes for the harbor porpoise.

Natural selection has transformed the shape and physiology of cetaceans, and this includes modifications to the five senses. Each species utilizes the senses to a greater or lesser extent depending upon habitat, selective pressures, and ancestry. The sense of

mals, has also evolved in cetaceans. Their smooth skin is highly specialized, its sensitivity enhanced by a vast network of nerve endings. The skin plays an important role in the whales' social life and their awareness of the environment surrounding them. Even the largest whales have a great sensitivity to gentle contact with other whales and touch seems to play a lifelong role in social interactions. The gentle brush of a flipper leading a newborn calf, the caress of a flipper or a fluke during courtship, or a strong and brutal push or shove during mating rituals are all common in the social life of whales. Their skin may be able to sense the air above the surface and inform the whale when to open their blowhole(s). The skin may also sense areas of different water pressure along the body and assist in changing the shape of the body in subtle ways to generate

Above: In an eruption of water, fish, and gaping mouths, a group of humpback whales feeds cooperatively at the surface. The rorqual grooves expand like an accordion as throats fill with water and prey. The sack-like tongue of the humpback whale turns inside out, lining the throat. Reverting the tongue pushes water through the baleen, capturing prey, which become a new meal for the hungry

whale. Humpback whales use a variety of hunting techniques to corral and confuse prey. Bubble nets and clouds are blown at depth to concentrate prey into a tight ball. Groups of whales sometimes work together to hunt and capture prey, with each individual whale playing a specific role.
Photo by Stephen Mullane

vision is very important to most whales to detect prey and predators, but also to recognize each other. Specialized muscles shape the lens so that whales can see equally well underwater and above the surface. To see in the surface bright light or in the darkened depths, the cetaceans' pupil is capable of a large range of dilation.

How a whale's sense of hearing functions is still a matter of discussion among many scientists. Baleen whales allow for the transmission of sound between water and their internal ear with the use of a horny wax plug in the external ear, which probably weakens their hearing above water. Toothed whales do not have a wax plug, but instead allow water to penetrate the ear canal thus allowing the transmission of sound between the water and the internal ear. Without water within the ear canal, toothed whales may have limited hearing above the surface. Scientists also believe that whales receive sounds transmitted underwater through the lower jaw which contains cavities filled with oil, channeling sound waves directly to the inner ear.

The sense of touch, very important in humans and other mam-

the best swimming output, or laminar flow, in order to reduce drag.

The sense of smell, important to many land mammals to detect food, predators, and one another, has undergone a dramatic change in cetaceans. As far as scientists have been able to establish, the sense of smell is very poor or nonexistent in most whales. Olfactory receptors are extremely limited and only the baleen whales may be able to "smell the wind" and detect the location of plankton-rich waters by sensing the airborne chemicals associated with them at the surface. The detection of waterborne chemicals seems to be possible through the whales' sense of taste. Dolphins in particular appear to have a well developed sense of taste, capable of discerning the quality of their food, and tasting the presence of other dolphins by detecting waste material, such as urine, decomposing in the water. This sense may play a role in their reproductive cycle, as males are able to detect the presence of sexual hormones present in the urine excreted in the water by sexually active females.

BALEEN WHALES

Baleen whales are members of the suborder Mysticeti. The word mysticeti means "mustached whale," in reference to the plates of baleen growing down from the roof of the mouth. There are anywhere from 100 to 420 baleen plates on each side of the upper jaw depending on the species. Baleen, also called "whalebone" by 19th century whalers, is made from the same keratin material as our fingernails and grows continuously throughout the life of the animal. A single plate consists of many fibers cemented together in a row. As the baleen grows, the interior portion next to the tongue becomes frayed, forming a mat of intertwined fibers. This mat acts as a filtering mechanism. Prey entering the mouth are trapped on the sieve-like surface as water flows around the fibers, between the plates and out of the mouth. Prey captured on the baleen are moved to the opening of the esophagus where they enter the digestive system.

Baleen whales share a number of characteristics. They all have two external blowholes, in contrast to toothed whales who have only one. Baleen whales, in general, migrate great distances between their summer feeding grounds and winter mating and calving areas.

They are very large animals; the smallest, the pygmy right whale, reaches lengths just over 20 feet (6 m). The suborder includes the longest whales, the blue and finback, and the most rotund, the bowhead and right whales. Baleen whales feed on schools or swarms of small prey, rather than catching a single prey at at a time like toothed whales. For this reason they have large heads and broad lower jaw bones that are separated for most of their length, whereas the lower jaws of toothed whales are fused for a considerable length. Their symmetrical head is large in order to support the long rows of baleen. The arched lower jaws allow large volumes of water and prey into the mouth and throat during feeding.

There are four families of baleen whales in the suborder Mysticeti, with at least one living species in each. The family Balaenidae contains the northern and southern right whales and the bowhead. The northern right whale is the only species of this group found along the East Coast. They are extremely large whales with long baleen and a strongly arched forward portion of the head. They lack a dorsal fin and have large broad pectoral flippers. They feed primarily on zooplankton, although the bowhead is known to feed on amphipods and other living organisms on the ocean bottom.

The Balaenopteridae family contains the long sleek baleen whales, such as the blue, finback, sei, minke, and the humpback which are all found in the North Atlantic and the Bryde's, which can be found in more equatorial waters. They are also known as rorqual whales. The balaenopterids have large straight heads with shorter and more coarse baleen. They have dorsal fins and are streamlined. They are fast swimmers, primarily feeding on swarms of krill and schools of small fish.

The other two baleen whale families each have a single member. The Neobalaenidae contains the pygmy right whale of southern oceans and the Eschrichtidae contains the gray whale of the North Pacific. Each has an interesting mix of characteristics. The pygmy right whale has an arched skull like the right whales, but possesses two throat grooves, a dorsal fin and a rostral ridge like rorqual

AN OCEAN OF PREY

The basis of nearly all marine food webs depends upon plankton. The plant-like plankton is called phytoplankton. Phyto means "light" and refers to photosynthesis, the process of using the energy from the sun to combine carbon dioxide and water to form simple sugars and oxygen. The animal plankton are called zooplankton and feed on the blooms of phytoplankton drifting in the oceans.

Phytoplankton are single celled algae, and like plants on land, require minerals to build their cells and sunlight to carry out photosynthesis. When the necessary amount of each is present, phytoplankton blooms quickly occur and the color of the water changes from winter blue to summer green. In cold polar waters plankton blooms can become so thick visibility is reduced to only a few feet.

Plankton blooms occur where nutrient-rich water rises to the upper, sunlit layer of the water column. Areas of upwelling occur where deep ocean currents strike continents, oceanic islands, or shallow banks. Tidal currents and strong winds can also create localized areas of mixing and currents can also concentrate plankton in areas where production is low. The discharge of minerals from freshwater rivers into coastal regions enhances seasonal plankton blooms especially in the Gulf of Maine and near the mouth of the Mississippi and St. Lawrence Rivers.

Zooplankton can reproduce rapidly in response to phytoplankton abundance. The zooplankton include many species of tiny crustaceans, the larvae of crabs, mollusks and fish, and the shrimp-like krill. Krill are a major food source for baleen whales and in the southern oceans surface patches of mating krill can extend over hundreds of square miles. The zooplankton provide a huge food supply for many species of schooling fish such as capelin, sand lance and herring. These schools of fish form another source of food for whales such as the finback, the minke, and the humpback as well as many toothed whales.

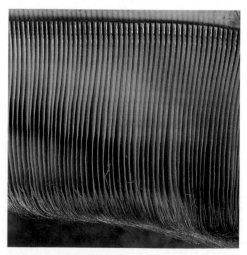

Left: Krill. This small animal resembling a shrimp is a major part of many baleen whales' diet.
Photo by Flip Nicklin / Minden Pictures

Above: Baleen of a Minke whale. Baleen whales are equipped with a series of keratin plates composed of fine bristles cemented together. The frayed interior edges of the baleen filter food from the water.
Photo by Stephen Mullane

whales. The gray whale has short coarse baleen, two to five throat grooves, and a dorsal hump rather than a dorsal fin. It feeds on concentrations of amphipods and other marine creatures found on the bottom. The coarse baleen is an adaptation for filtering prey from the mud and water that enter the mouth while feeding.

The length of the baleen plates and the coarseness of the filter-

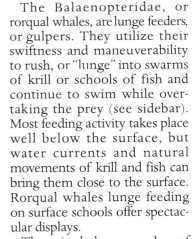

ing mat vary from one species to the next. Bowhead whales from the North Pacific have baleen reaching 12 feet (3.66 m) in length. The frayed baleen fibers are long and thin forming a fine mat that is almost silky in texture. In right whales, the baleen plates reach 9 feet (3 m) and have a fine filtering surface like the bowhead's. The spaces between the interwoven fibers are small enough to catch tiny zooplankton that are no larger than grains of rice. The rorqual whales have shorter and coarser baleen. They feed on krill and fish. The sei whale and the minke whale, the smallest whale of the rorqual group, have fairly fine baleen and feed on small zooplankton, as well as krill and fish.

Baleen whales have evolved to take advantage of the abundant concentrations of copepods, amphipods, krill, and a variety of schooling fish found in cold polar waters. The shape of their bodies, daily activity, seasonal migrations, and feeding behavior have been influenced by the search for food; each prey species necessitating a different set of physical and behavioral adaptations.

In general, there are three major feeding techniques used by baleen whales: bottom feeding, lunge feeding, and skim-feeding. Gray whales are mostly bottom feeders, and there is evidence that bowheads and some humpbacks feed occasionally on the bottom as well. Bowheads and right whales are skim-feeders. When they find a concentration of copepods, they swim along with their

mouths open. Water entering the front of the mouth exits through the baleen and out the corner of the jaw. The zooplankton trapped on the baleen mat is scraped off by the tongue and swallowed. On calm summer days right whales are occasionally seen skim-feeding at the surface with a portion of their rostrum and baleen showing above the water.

The Balaenopteridae, or rorqual whales, are lunge feeders, or gulpers. They utilize their swiftness and maneuverability to rush, or "lunge" into swarms of krill or schools of fish and continue to swim while overtaking the prey (see sidebar). Most feeding activity takes place well below the surface, but water currents and natural movements of krill and fish can bring them close to the surface. Rorqual whales lunge feeding on surface schools offer spectacular displays.

The sei whale, a member of the rorqual family, has been observed skim-feeding as well, swimming just under the surface with its mouth open. Using its finer baleen bristles it is able to filter smaller prey, such as copepods and krill.

Left: A northern right whale skim-feeding. With its mouth open it moves forward, filtering small zooplankton from the water. Sensitive to changing prey concentrations, right whales, despite their bulk, can turn rapidly to stay within in a patch of food.
Photo by François Gohier

Above: Finback whale lunge feeding. Notice the lunge being done with the right side of the face and jaw facing the prey. It is possible that the finback uses the white coloration on that side of the face to concentrate prey. The throat grooves, typical of the rorqual family of baleen whales, are evident.
Photo by Michael S. Nolan / Seapics

RORQUAL WHALES

The family Balaenopteridae, or rorqual whales, is composed of six species in two genera. The blue whale, the sei whale, the finback whale, the minke whale, and the Bryde's whale are members of the genus Balaenoptera. The humpback whale is in the genus Megaptera.

The word "rorqual" comes from the old Norse language composed of "ror" for furrow or groove, and "val" standing for whale. These refer to the long parallel throat grooves extending in rorqual whales from the lips to between the back of the flippers and the umbilicus. Numbering up to one hundred, these grooves expand as the whale feeds to allow for a huge quantity of water and food to enter the mouth cavity. Once fully expanded, these grooves contract and expel the water against the inside wall of the baleen plates. The food collected and filtered by the baleen is directed to the esophagus by the tongue and then ingested.

This remarkable system allows for the capture and filtration of the huge amount of food required for the growth and sustenance of the rorqual whales.

All rorqual whales, except for the Bryde's whale, which remains most of the year in warmer waters, are exceptional travelers, migrating thousands of miles every year between cold-water summer feeding grounds and warmer winter reproductive grounds. When actively feeding, they must ingest huge quantities of food every day in the rich feeding grounds to store reserves in their layer of blubber. These reserves are used during months of migrations and lean times, as well as in the production of fat-rich milk for the nutrition of newborn calves. A blue whale may take up to 45 metric tons of water in one mouthful and retain about 4 tons (3,600 kg) of food each day. The much smaller minke whale is known to ingest about 80 to 320 lbs (40-145 kg) of food per day during their feeding season.

The presence and role of throat grooves is made even more efficient with the use of very specialized hunting and feeding techniques such as lunge feeding, gulping, and skimming, as well the very unique feeding techniques of the humpbacks known as bubblenet feeding (see humpback text).

Toothed Whales

Already graceful, a baby Atlantic spotted dolphin (Stenella frontalis) jumps alongside his mother. The young are grey at birth. They become spotted as they reach maturity. They are avid bow-riders and will stay in the company of ships for miles to catch the free ride offered by their bow waves.
Photo by Brandon D. Cole

Toothed whales form a very diverse group. Feeding on a single fish or squid, they are not limited, like baleen whales, to regions that support vast schools of fish and krill. They have evolved to exploit many marine habitats, from warm tropical waters to the ice-filled polar seas, from the deep ocean basins to shallow continental coastlines. Others have evolved to take advantage of the environment provided by some freshwater rivers. They range in size from the tiny 5-foot porpoises to the 60-foot sperm whale. About seventy species have been found throughout the world and more are being discovered. Some are seen regularly by inhabitants of coastal waters and well known by the scientific community, while others have never been seen alive and are known only by bones found washed up on a beach.

Toothed whales are members of the cetacean suborder Odontoceti. While all have teeth, the number, size, and shape varies greatly. In dolphins the teeth are the same, or homodont, from the front of the jaw to the back. Some oceanic dolphins have more than forty conical teeth on either side of the upper and lower jaws, while many beaked whales have only two.

Most toothed whales have a single nasal passage opening in a single blowhole, the only exception being the sperm whale which has two nasal passages opening in a common blowhole. Most toothed whales have a dorsal fin. They tend to be smaller than baleen whales, but the sperm whale, killer whale, bottlenose whale (not to be confused with the bottlenose dolphin), and some beaked whales, all reach lengths of about 30 feet or more. Most species live in tightly knit social groups of various sizes and many feed in groups, coordinating their

movements to herd prey. In general, they do not migrate long distances, but some oceanic dolphins roam widely across the sea, and male sperm whales migrate between separate feeding and mating grounds.

Like bats, odontocetes have a highly developed echolocation system allowing them to catch prey in the dark, in murky water, or even hiding in the sand. The melon, a fatty sac-like structure, cradled by the bones of the upper skull and jaw, is characteristic of all toothed whales. The melon and other associated modifications of the air passages, lower jaw bone, and ear structures, have evolved in concert, refining the toothed whales' sonar capabilities.

Highly social, many toothed whales produce a wide variety of sounds that may be used in communication. Many have evolved anatomical and physiological features that allow them to dive to incredible depths in search of prey.

The suborder is broken into nine families, three of which include the five different river dolphins. Representatives of the remaining six families are found along the eastern seaboard of North America, some venturing only to the continental shelf break.

The sperm whale is in the family Physeteridae and is characterized by its large blunt head and small underslung lower jaw. Adapted to the open ocean, sperm whales dive to tremendous depths of 6,500 feet (2,000 meters) or more. The dwarf sperm whale and the pygmy sperm whale are in the family Kogia. They are small whales, growing to around 10 to 12 feet

Left: A white-sided dolphin leaping above the waters of the Gulf of Maine just off Mount Desert Rock. Leaping dolphins are a true joy to see. Frequently riding the bow of boats and ships, dolphins have provided company and inspired mariners for centuries.
Photo by Stephen Mullane

Right: The consummate predator, the beautiful killer whale, or Orca, erupts above the surface. Orcas are among the largest of the toothed whales. They roam the seas of the world in search of many different prey species, including large whales.
Photo by Brandon D. Cole

(3 to 3.7 m). They have large heads, but not proportionately as large as the sperm whale. Rarely seen alive, they frequently strand along the southeastern coast of the United States, and occasionally northwards into Labrador.

The family Ziphiidae contains seventeen species of the little-known beaked whales and two species of bottlenose whales. They are deep divers that feed on many species of cephalopods (squid, octopus, and cuttlefish). Very little is known about beaked whales. They are rarely observed at sea and are difficult to identify. Much of what is known is based upon stranded specimens. Many have only two teeth in the lower jaw. Beaked whales have long irregular scars on their bodies suggesting battles between rivals. Females may never have functional teeth as adults. The presence of two throat grooves suggests they are suction feeders. The bottlenose whales

have pronounced beaks, bulbous heads, and grow to 29 feet (9 m). A small population lives year round in an underwater canyon known as "The Gully" off the coast of Nova Scotia. Their repetitive deep dives place them next to sperm whales in diving ability.

The family Monodontidae includes the beluga and the narwhal. These are whales of the Arctic Ocean, often associated with pack ice. The cervical vertebrae in both species are unfused permitting rotation of the head, especially in the beluga whale. Male narwhals grow spiral tusks 6 to 10 feet in length (2 to 3 meters). These are used in dominance displays between males, possibly affecting mating success.

The family Delphinidae is the most diverse and familiar group of toothed whales. The family includes the dolphins, the orca and false killer whale, and the pilot

ECHOLOCATION

Visibility is limited underwater and whales often forage at night, or at depths where light does not penetrate. Toothed whales have overcome these challenges by developing a way to use sound to detect, or "see" objects in limited visibility. This is known as echolocation.

By producing high frequency pulsed sounds, or clicks, and interpreting the echoes bouncing off objects in the water, toothed whales are able to avoid obstacles and to locate prey. The interpretation can be highly sensitive. Bottlenose

focus the sounds as they exit the head.

When these sound pulses strike an object of a different density an echo is reflected back to the whale. They are received by the whale through the lower jaw, which contains a fat filled cavity, conducting sounds to the middle and inner ear. The brains of toothed whales are highly developed, especially those regions associated with the processing of acoustical data.

Toothed whales are able to discern which

objects in the water. Some researchers have speculated that dolphins may be able to "see" the internal organs, bones, and air passages of group members, prey, and other creatures swimming with them. It is also possible that toothed whales are able to determine whether group members are ill by discerning anatomical differences, and even notice if females in the group are pregnant.

Longer wavelength clicks are used while the toothed whales swim in more open water. As

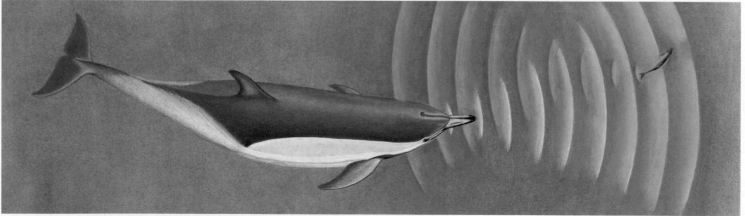

dolphins in captivity have shown the ability to detect the difference in identically shaped objects made from different materials.

Toothed whales have developed many anatomical structures associated with the use of sound for echolocation. The sounds are probably produced by air movements in the trachea and tissues of the nasal sacs and passages next to the blowhole. These sounds, heard as clicks, are produced in a series called a train. The clicks are then reflected forward by the skull through the fatty melon, located above the upper jaw. The melon and the skull bones act as an acoustical lens and help channel and

echo is associated with which click, and by interpreting the delay in the echo's return they are able to determine the distance to an object. Objects of different sizes and densities produce echoes of different intensity and quality, adding to the complexity and potential accuracy of the interpretation.

While dolphins swim through the water they modulate the frequency, or wavelength, of the echolocating clicks. The range of sounds produced includes sounds well above and well below what humans can hear. Shorter wavelength sounds help distinguish smaller objects, the details of their surface, but also details within

they approach objects, the frequency rises, increasing the detail and the amount of information available for interpretation. Lower frequency sounds are used to identify objects at greater distances, as they are capable of traveling out and back without being lost in the background noise always present in the ocean.

Because baleen whales are known for their low frequency and ultra-low frequency sounds capable of traveling hundreds even thousands of miles below the ocean's surface, it is thought that baleen whales also use low frequency sounds for navigation and to "see" the ocean floor topography.

whales. Dolphins have many pointed conical teeth and most have an elongated beak protruding from the bulbous head or melon. Most species have curved dorsal fins, although the rightwhale dolphins of the Pacific lack one. In contrast the Phocoeniids, or porpoises, have flattened spade-shaped teeth and indistinct, more rounded beaks. They are small whales with short triangular-shaped dorsal fins.

Several species of dolphins are common along the East Coast. Bottlenose dolphins inhabit coastal bays and estuaries from the Florida Keys north to the Chesapeake Bay, and can frequently be seen from shore, especially in Florida. Common, spotted and striped dolphins can be seen along the continental slope and shelf break south of New England. Pilot whales are common offshore all along the continental shelf, from Florida to the Canadian Maritimes.

The largest concentrations and number of species of toothed whales along our coast are found where the relatively shallow continental shelf slopes steeply into the deep ocean basin. It is here, where the bottom drops from 300 to 6,000 feet (100 to 2,000 meters) and beyond in a few miles, that a multitude of prey can be found, as well as the whales that feed upon them.

Because of competition for the resources available, cetacean species have evolved to take advantage of many different environments and to hunt for prey in many different ways and at different depths. It is not uncommon to venture east off the coast of Virginia in the spring, to the outer continental shelf and shelf break, and find a remarkable diversity of whales in a small area. Pods of sperm, pilot, and grampus whales (also named Risso's dolphins) can be seen, with a

Harbor porpoise and the robust white-sided and white-beaked dolphins are common in the cooler waters of the North Atlantic. Killer whales are also found occasionally throughout the region.

Toothed whales organize themselves in many different social groups, often centered around females. Long-lasting family groups center upon older females and their offspring. Adult males occasionally move from group to group during mating season. In some species mature males leave the family groups to form small groups of their own, or in the case of the sperm whale, the older males live solitary lives except during breeding season.

Family groups offer a wide range of advantages. Skills and information are passed from one generation to the next, especially when multiple generations exist within a group. When several adult females with offspring live within a group, they often share the care for young members of the group at the surface, while other mothers dive for food. Large family groups improve the chances of finding food and the ability to detect and protect one another from predators.

number of beaked whales scattered here and there in between. Huge herds of common dolphins pass by, and smaller groups of bottlenose, spotted, and striped dolphins weave their way through this cetacean gathering. During the summer months various species of squid and fish move up onto the continental shelf in pursuit of prey and to breed. A number of toothed whale species follow this migration, while others will remain offshore.

Left: A bottlenose dolphin uses echolocation to locate food hidden under the sand. Toothed whales use their highly developed sense of echolocation to locate prey under many different conditions and to take advantage of many different habitats, from murky silt laden rivers, to the ink black depths thousands of feet below the surface.
Photo by Doug Perrine / Seapics

Above: A pair of common dolphins cruising at high speed along with a white-sided dolphin. Highly social animals, dolphins live in extended family groups and are often seen in association with other toothed whales and baleen whales.
Photo by Robin W. Baird / Marine Mammal Images

FIELD IDENTIFICATIONS OF LARGER WHALES

To spend any time near the oceans or at sea searching for whales, it is helpful to know what to look for and how to differentiate species. As it is never guaranteed that whales will approach close to shore or to a vessel to allow for observation and positive identification, it is important to pick up every detail possible when the whales are at the surface, even if it is a mile away. The height and shape of the spout, the presence or absence of a dorsal fin, the length of time at the surface, and whether a fluke is lifted from the water at the end of a series of breaths, are important characteristics to look for initially. If whales approach, the size, the shape of the head and dorsal fin, and the color of the underside of the flukes will be more apparent and thus become useful. Closer glimpses will reveal finer details such as the color of the skin, the pres-

ence of skin parasites, and the contour of the fluke's trailing edge.

The weather, the often changing sea conditions, the direction the whale is traveling, and the location of the sun in reference to the whale and the observer will affect visibility and contrast, as well as spout height and shape. Moderate to brisk wind will knock the spout down, turning the tall spout of a fin whale into something resembling a humpback's. Wind and waves can also obscure bodies, dorsal fins, and flukes.

It takes a seasoned whale observer many years in the field to acquire the experience necessary to be able to identify each species accurately under a variety of conditions. With patience and perseverance the whale watcher will be able to identify the species observed, and in time, what to expect when at sea.

FINBACK WHALE

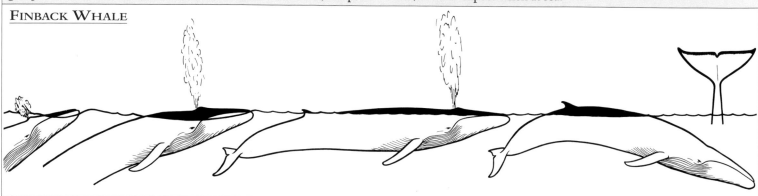

The Spout:
The spout reaches 15 to 20 feet (4 to 6 meters) and is rather tall and narrow.

Dive Sequence:
Fast moving, 5 to 15 blows with 10 to 30 seconds between each breath. Then dives for a duration of 5 to 15 minutes.

Top of head and blowholes emerge first. The whale blows while remaining low in the water. Following the blow the long back appears, with the tall dorsal fin.

On the last breath, back and dorsal fin arch high out of the water showing upper tail stock. The fin-back rarely flukes. Look for a white coloration on the

lower right jaw. This can sometimes be observed while the whale moves just below the surface between breaths. Often erratic and elusive, appearing consid-

erable distances from last known position and in opposite direction of last known heading. It is seen alone or in small groups.

HUMPBACK WHALE

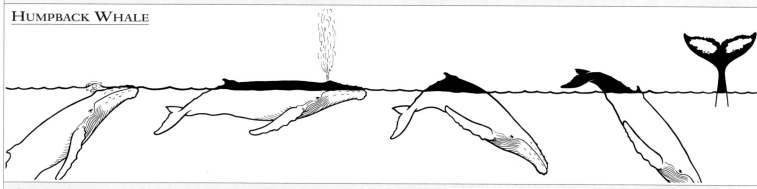

The Spout:
The spout is highly visible, bushy and somewhat pear-shaped. Reaches 10 to 15 feet (3 to 5 meters).

Dive Sequence:
Slow dive sequence. Has 5 to 12 blows, separated by about 10 to 30 seconds. Dives will last from 5 to 12 minutes.

First to be seen are the blowholes and splash-guards. The body contin-ues to surface and a stub-by dorsal fin appears. Body then slowly arches

with an increasingly large triangular form above sur-face known as the "hump". The dorsal fin re-enters the water as the tail stock arch-es further. The tail stock

lowers to the surface and the flukes are lifted clear of the water. Trailing edges of flukes are ragged, the underneath surface varies from white to black.

Disproportionately large white flippers are often noticeable below surface. Has an active surface behavior. Found alone or in groups.

SEI WHALE

The Spout:
Somewhat bushy spout, similar to finback but not as tall. Reaches 10 to 15 feet (3 to 5 meters).

Dive Sequence:
5 to 15 blows at surface, followed by a 5 to 10-minute dive. Head rises at shallow angle. Blowholes and dorsal fin usually

reach surface nearly simultaneously, unlike finback or blue. The back and dorsal fin will contin-ue to appear at surface for awhile. The dorsal fin is

tall and falcate in shape, angular along trailing edge. Slight arch of back before dive, but no arching of tail stock usually visi-ble. The fluke does not

appear at or above surface during the dive sequence. Look for absence of white lower right jaw to differ-entiate from finback whale's obvious markings.

Look for "footprints" (cir-cles of slick water) on sur-face of water as whale swims just below the sur-face, "ghosting" along.

BLUE WHALE

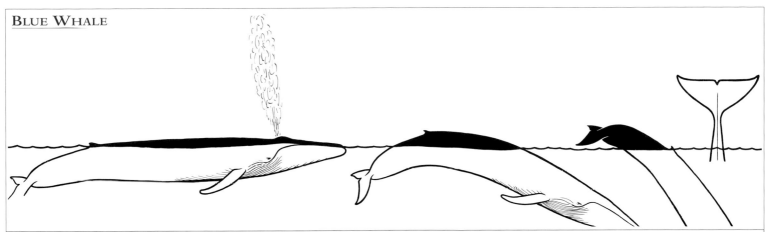

The Spout:
Spout of all spouts. Columnar and tall. Can reach 15 to 30 feet (4.5 to 9 meters) sometimes higher.

Dive Sequence:
Will have 5 to 15 blows at surface followed by a dive lasting 5 to 20 minutes. Usually will appear at surface at low angle. After large blow the head lowers underwater and the very long body begins to roll. The small dorsal fin, 3/4 of the way back on body then appears. Dorsal fin is much smaller than finback whale. Back continues to roll and arches slowly before dive. Tail stock may or may not arch. Very broad flukes are then raised, but not always. The flukes then disappear below water. Look for broad flat rostrum and large "splashguards", beautiful mottled skin coloration, and yellow diatom growth on skin. Can be solitary or in small groups. The large size usually leaves little doubt on the identity of this largest of all whales.

MINKE WHALE

The Spout:
Difficult to see, mostly absent, but can be heard. Will reach 4 to 8 feet (1 ½ to 2 ½ meters).

Dive Sequence:
The minke is fast moving. Appears 2 to 4 times at the surface 30 to 60 seconds apart. Then dives for a duration of 2 to 6 minutes. The jaw and rostrum emerge at an angle before the body flattens and the blowholes appear. The back and highly curved dorsal fin then appear. Before the dive, the back and dorsal fin begin to arch, and the tail stock arches as well. Does not fluke up. Minkes usually appear alone and swim erratically, often changing directions between surfacing. Seen at the perimeter of groups of larger whales. Look for white flipper patches as minke surfaces nearby. Approaches close to rocky shorelines and enters bays and harbors.

NORTHERN RIGHT WHALE

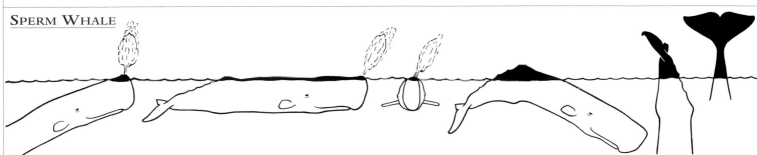

The Spout:
Very bushy and wide. Has a classic "V" shape clearly perceptible when seen from fore and aft. Reaches 8 to 12 feet (2 to 4 meters).

Dive Sequence:
Slow. Takes 5 to 15 breaths. Dives will last 10 to 30 minutes, sometimes more. Rounded head appears high above surface. If close, callosities can be clearly seen; typical on rostrum, chin, and above eyes. No dorsal fin is present. As the body continues to roll, the broad, large triangular flukes appear. The flukes have a smooth trailing edge with a deep median notch. The flukes are lifted on terminal dive. Many have white rope scars on tips and along leading edge of flukes. The flukes then disappear as the whale sinks at a vertical angle. They often surface after a long dive in the same locations as last series of breaths. This may occur even when a fast current is present. Look for callosities and cyamids on whale.

SPERM WHALE

The Spout:
Spout is low and bushy, projected at an angle slightly forward and to the left. About 4 to 5 feet high (1.3 to 1.8 meters) but about 8 to 12 feet long (2.5 to 3.6 meters).

Dive Sequence:
Will have up to 60 blows at surface. They will dive for about 5 to 60 minutes or longer. Often resurface at the same spot. The whale will lift head above water for final blow and breath. Body is lowered sometimes entirely under water. The whale then reappears moving faster. The "nubby" dorsal fin appears. Back begins to arch, and if close, skin wrinkles are visible. Behind dorsal fin, bumps on caudal ridge appear. On terminal dive flukes and large portion of rear of the body are lifted high above surface. Trailing edge of flukes are irregular. Adult males are usually solitary. Sperm whale is often seen "logging" at the surface, resting between breaths, awash in the waves.

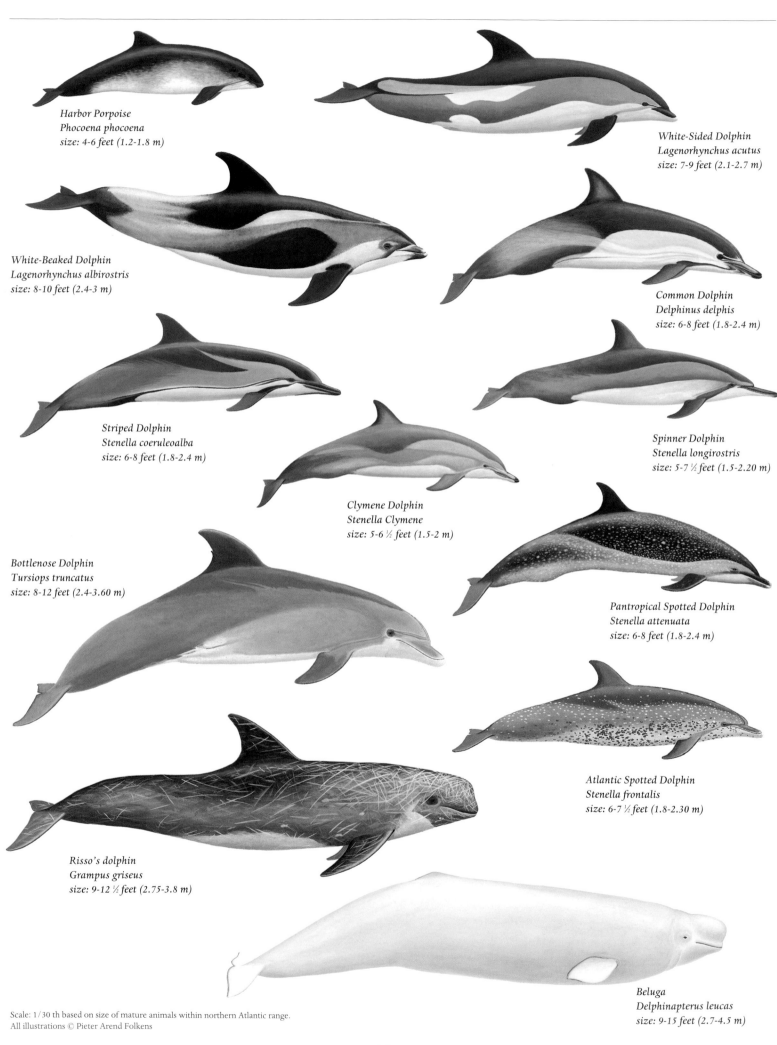

Harbor Porpoise
Phocoena phocoena
size: 4-6 feet (1.2-1.8 m)

White-Sided Dolphin
Lagenorhynchus acutus
size: 7-9 feet (2.1-2.7 m)

White-Beaked Dolphin
Lagenorhynchus albirostris
size: 8-10 feet (2.4-3 m)

Common Dolphin
Delphinus delphis
size: 6-8 feet (1.8-2.4 m)

Striped Dolphin
Stenella coeruleoalba
size: 6-8 feet (1.8-2.4 m)

Spinner Dolphin
Stenella longirostris
size: 5-7 ½ feet (1.5-2.20 m)

Clymene Dolphin
Stenella Clymene
size: 5-6 ½ feet (1.5-2 m)

Bottlenose Dolphin
Tursiops truncatus
size: 8-12 feet (2.4-3.60 m)

Pantropical Spotted Dolphin
Stenella attenuata
size: 6-8 feet (1.8-2.4 m)

Atlantic Spotted Dolphin
Stenella frontalis
size: 6-7 ½ feet (1.8-2.30 m)

Risso's dolphin
Grampus griseus
size: 9-12 ½ feet (2.75-3.8 m)

Beluga
Delphinapterus leucas
size: 9-15 feet (2.7-4.5 m)

Scale: 1/30 th based on size of mature animals within northern Atlantic range.
All illustrations © Pieter Arend Folkens

Above: The silence of a summer evening in the northern Gulf of Maine is momentarily shattered by three humpback whales feeding on surface schooling herring.
Coordinated feeding efforts help corral fish into densely packed "balls" where fish and water are engulfed in the whales' mouths and expandable throats.
Photo by Stephen Mullane

WATCHING WHALES AND DOLPHINS FROM THE EAST COAST

Species:	Best Places:	Best Time:
Finback Whale:	Continental shelf Cape Hatteras to Greenland. Locally common: Long Island, Cape Cod Bay, Gulf of Maine, Bay of Fundy, Gulf of St. Lawrence, Newfoundland.	From mid-April to mid-November north. Some individuals even in winter. Year-round off Long Island.
Minke Whale:	Mid-Atlantic Coast, Cape Cod, Gulf of Maine north to Newfoundland and also in eastern Gulf of Mexico.	Winter and spring along Mid-Atlantic, Long island and Cape Cod Bay in spring, Gulf of Maine in summer and fall.
Sei Whale:	Occasionally in Cape Cod Bay and Gulf of Maine, Bay of Fundy and coast off Nova Scotia (unpredictable), Newfoundland and Labrador.	Summer in Gulf of Maine. Spring, summer and fall off Nova Scotia.
Blue Whale:	Gulf of St. Lawrence, St. Lawrence and Saguenay River estuary.	Spring, summer, and fall.
Humpback Whale:	Continental shelf Chesapeake Bay north to Greenland. Especially Cape Cod Bay, Massachusetts, New Hampshire and Maine. Bay of Fundy, Gulf of St.Lawrence, and Newfoundland. Some winter off of Virginia.	Spring through late fall, some winter near Cape Cod. Winter.
Northern Right Whale:	Cape Cod Bay north to Bay of Fundy. Florida, Georgia, and Carolinas' coast.	Spring, summer, and fall. Some in Cape Cod bay in winter. Winter.
Sperm Whale:	Offshore in deep water along the continental shelf slope and open ocean. From the Gulf of Mexico to polar ice.	Spring, summer, and fall, mid-Atlantic states north along shelf edge. Year-round in the Gulf of Mexico.
White-Sided Dolphin:	Cape Cod Bay, Gulf of Maine, Georges Bank north to Newfoundland, Gulf of St.Lawrence.	Spring, summer, and fall. Some winter near Cape Cod.
White-Beaked Dolphin:	Occasionally in the Gulf of Maine south to Cape Cod. More numerous in the Gulf of St. Lawrence and Newfoundland.	Spring to fall, fewer sightings in the Gulf of Maine recently.
Common Dolphin:	Gulf of Mexico north to Newfoundland, found along the continental shelf slope.	Year-round south, in summer on Georges Banks north along Nova Scotia to Newfoundland.
Bottlenose Dolphin:	Gulf of Mexico, Florida north to Long Island.	Year-round in Gulf of Mexico, coastal Florida north to Cape Hatteras. Seen in summer all the way to Long Island and New Jersey coast.
Harbor Porpoise:	Cape Hatteras to Greenland. Most numerous and seen from shore in Gulf of Maine and Bay of Fundy. Good numbers in Gulf of St. Lawrence.	Spring, summer, and fall.
Pilot Whales:	Short-finned: Gulf of Mexico north to New York. Long-finned: North Carolina north to Greenland, in Gulf of St. Lawrence local populations can be seen from shore.	Year round in southern areas of range. Along shelf slope in winter and across shelf in summer, occasional in Cape Cod Bay and Gulf of Maine in summer and fall.
Beluga Whale:	St. Lawrence and Saguenay Rivers, Gulf of St. Lawrence.	Spring, summer, and fall.
Killer Whale:	Gulf of Mexico north to Greenland if your lucky. Occasionally in summer and fall in Gulf of Maine and Bay of Fundy.	Spring, summer, and fall, more common north.
Striped Dolphin:	Similar to common dolphin, associated with continental slope and open ocean.	Year-round along slope waters, Gulf of Mexico to mid-Atlantic states, north in summer.
Spotted Dolphin:	Coastal and oceanic populations from Gulf of Mexico and Caribbean to Chesapeake Bay.	Year-round south of Cape Hatteras along shore outward. In summer over shelf to Cape Cod and Georges Bank.
Spinner Dolphin:	Oceanic basins and along edges of continental shelf. Gulf of mexico north to New Jersey.	Year-round in northern Gulf of Mexico and west of Florida.
Clymene Dolphin:	Range overlaps spinner dolphin in Atlantic, Northern Gulf of mexico, and Caribbean.	Year-round.
Risso's Dolphin:	South of Georges Bank to Mid-Atlantic states. Gulf of Mexico.	Year-round off Georges Bank and Gulf of Mexico. In summer north to Newfoundland.
Beaked Whales:	Oceanic and deep ocean trenches. Southeast edge of Georges Bank. The "Gully" area, east of Nova Scotia for bottlenose whale.	Spring, summer, and fall off georges Bank. Year-round in Gulf of Mexico.

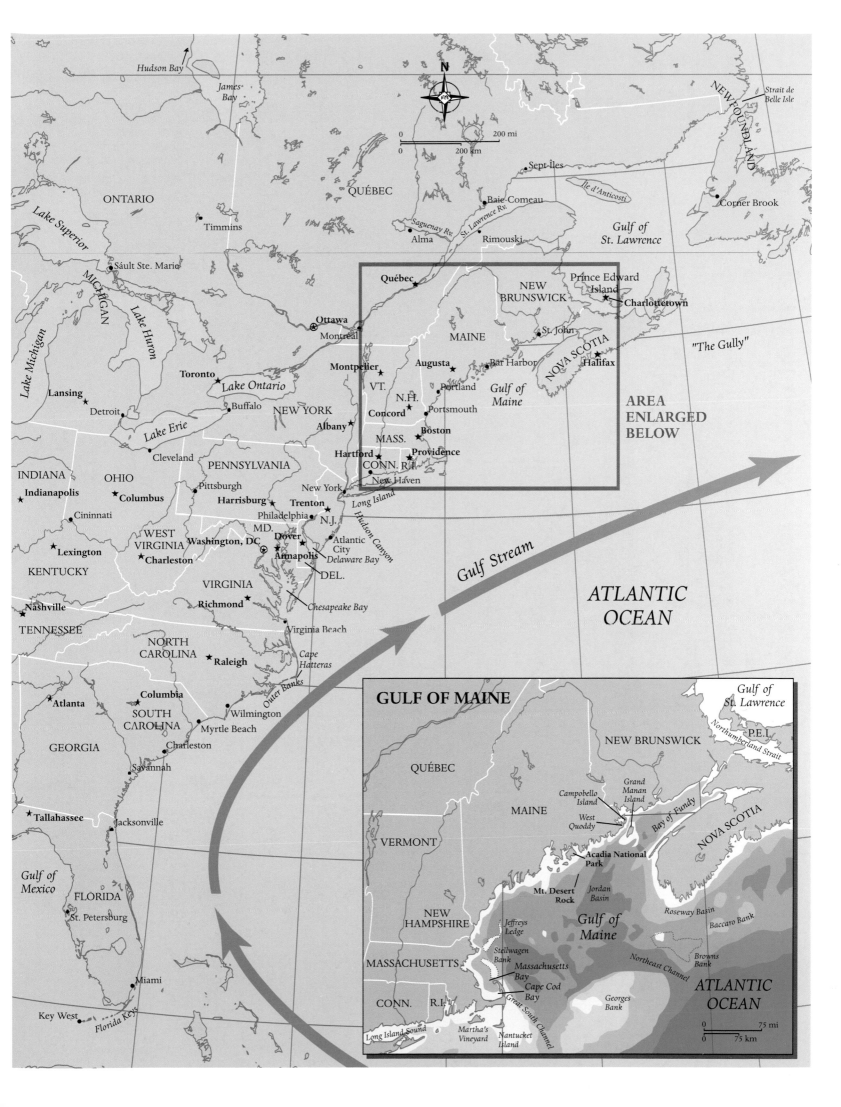

THE FINBACK WHALE

Found in all oceans of the world, finback whales (*Balaenoptera physalus*) are present throughout the North Atlantic. They are the most commonly seen large baleen whale along the continental shelf of the United States. They are named for the prominent dorsal fin, often reaching a height of two feet, which is situated two-thirds of the way back on the body.

The spout of the finback whale is columnar and tall, reaching twenty or more feet (6 m) on calm days. Finback whales breathe five to fifteen times in a row diving a short distance below the surface between each breath. After each breath they raise their back and their dorsal fin higher out of the water. After the last breath they arch their backs raising their dorsal fin five to six feet above the water, exposing a large section of the tail stock or caudal peduncle. Unlike humpbacks, finback whales generally do not raise their flukes. After a breathing sequence and "terminal dive," they stay down from five to fifteen minutes, often surfacing a half mile away and sometimes in the opposite direction from their last heading. They seem elusive and erratic, but their great size, prominent dorsal fin, and tall spouts make them easy to find.

The second largest of the great whales after the blue whale, mature finback whales can grow up to 85 feet (25.5 m) in length and reach weights between 50 and 70 tons (45,300 to 63,500 kg). Females are sexually mature around 60 feet (18 m), males slightly smaller. Sexually mature at six years, females produce calves every three years, sometimes every other year. Mating occurs mid-winter; calves are born after a gestation of 11 to 12 months. Calves are 20 feet (6 m) at birth and are weaned seven months later after growing another 16 feet.

The finback whale is known in all the oceans of the world, and is the most common great whale in the western North Atlantic. It can be seen alone or in small groups. The second largest baleen whale after the mighty blue whale, the finback can reach lengths of up to 85 feet (25.5 m). Finback whales feed on small schooling fish and shrimp-like euphausids known as krill. In the western North Atlantic finback whales return to the same summer feeding grounds year after year. Finback whales are all business. Constantly on the move in search of food, they show little interest in boats, unlike the sometimes curious humpback.
Photo by Michael S. Nolan / Seapics

Females with calves are seen in the spring and early summer from the coast of Maryland to the Gulf of Maine. In the Gulf of Maine, calves are more frequently sighted in the south, on Stellwagen Bank off Cape Cod, north to Jeffreys Ledge off New Hampshire. Where they mate and give birth is unknown; it is thought to be offshore in temperate to tropical waters.

Finback whales are light grey to black above, and creamy white below. The ventral surfaces of the flukes and the flippers are also white. Finbacks have an unusual asymmetrical skin coloration. The lower right jaw is white rather than the steel grey to black of the left jaw and back. Even the first third of the baleen plates on the right side of the mouth are yellowish white. This coloration sweeps up over the right side of the animal in a unique pattern that quickly changes from white to lighter shades of grey, finally fading into the normal slate grey of the back. These swirls and streaks look like comet tails spray painted on their skin. They also have a "V", or chevron shaped coloration, with the apex forward, situated on the midline behind the blowholes.

No one knows for sure why the right jaw is colored this way. Some have speculated that it may be used to concentrate prey into dense patches. They frequently roll at the surface with mouths agape, the right side down. How they feed below the surface is unknown. Whether this pigmentation is of use as camouflage, or to corral fish in the semi-darkness remains a mystery.

Left: A close-up view of a finback blow. Rising occasionally to 20 feet (6m), the blow of a finback whale can be seen for many miles under ideal conditions. On calm days spouting whales can be heard over a mile away, indicative of the tremendous force and speed of the exhalation.
Photo by François Gohier

Right: A rare finback whale breach. Breaching whales are an impressive sight and a thrilling experience, unfortunately the action is often over before the observer realizes what is happening.
Photo by Kirsten Young/Marine Mammal Images

Finback whales tend to be solitary in nature, forming small associations of two to three individuals for part of a day, a few hours, or for just a few minutes at the surface. Researchers define an association as two or more individuals moving together at the surface within one and a half body lengths of one another. Finback whales can communicate with one another over great distances. It is thought that they are able to produce sounds that travel hundreds, even thousands of miles underwater. This being the case, finbacks many miles apart may consider themselves associated with one another, while researchers are unaware of the presence of the faraway individuals.

When a particularly large source of food is located, finback whales may gather in loose groups of 50 or more individuals spread out over 20 to 40 square miles (51 to 103 km²). This may seem like a large area, but if in the middle of it, the observer feels surrounded with whales spouting and diving in all directions. It is an exhilarating sight!

In the Gulf of St. Lawrence, the Bay of Fundy, and off Long Island, finback whales have been observed moving in pods of 5 to 10 whales which together seem to form a larger cohesive group. These larger groups are observed moving in and out of feeding areas in unison. The nature of these groups raises many questions. Are they family groups, single sex bands, or individuals of the same age-class?

In the Gulf of Maine, researchers have observed finback whales form groups of 5 to 10 animals, usually in the late summer and fall. These groups swim closely together, charging out of the water at great speeds, with some whales rolling at the surface showing flippers, flukes, and occasionally aggressive male sexual displays. These "chase" or "rowdy" groups, as they are sometimes called, may be engaged in some type of sexual activity, possibly dominance displays, that are precursors to mating later in the season, or in life. The sexual composition of these groups are not known as they form quickly, do not last long, are very fast and erratic in movement, and difficult, even dangerous to approach. Much field work and genetic sampling

is still required to discover some of the details of these associations.

Finback whales feed upon euphausids, or krill, and locally abundant schooling fish such as capelin, herring, and sand lance. Over the shelf waters they feed throughout the water column from the surface down to 600 feet (180 m). Occasionally they can be seen feeding at the surface where they typically roll on their sides while engulfing a section of water and food. They are very rarely observed using bubble clouds, like humpback whales, to concentrate or disorient schooling fish. This behavior is limited to a few individual finback whales. One evening I watched a pair of finbacks feeding at the surface on 5 to 6 inch (10 to 12cm) long herring. The whales surfaced to breathe within 20 feet (6 m) of one another and dove. After 5 to 7 minutes there was an eruption of small fish on the water's surface. Only seconds later, the whales burst from the water with mouths wide open to engulf the fish along with a large section of water. After closing their mouths and contracting their throat muscles to expel the water, trapping the fish against their baleen, they rolled at the surface, breathed several times together, and dove for another run. For 30 to 90 seconds clouds of large bubbles could be seen rising in their feeding wake. Meanwhile, within a 4 mile (6.5 km) circle, 15 to 20

Above: Two finback whales lunge feeding. The oversized throats, filled with water, are clearly visible and show the large amount of water being trapped by the expanding rorqual grooves. They have up to 100 grooves depending on the whale's size. Finback whales use powerful bursts of speed to overtake schools of prey.
Photo by Carlos Navarro / Seapics

Left: A large finback diving in the waters of the Gulf of Maine. Mount Desert Island, Maine and Acadia National Park are seen in the distance. Found throughout the Atlantic, finback whales congregate across the continental shelf to feed. Many popular feeding grounds are within a short boat ride from shore, offering interested whale watchers the opportunity to see these magnificent animals in the wild.
Photo by Stephen Mullane

other finbacks went about their business, surfacing only to breathe.

Some patches of prey may exist over several square miles for a number of weeks before moving off or before being consumed and dispersed by the feeding whales and predatory fish. Groups of 20 to 30 finback whales have been seen feasting on large schools of herring within 120 feet (36 m) of the surface, while other finbacks 5 to 6 miles away (8 to 9.5 km) are found diving repeatedly upon very small patches of feed 300 feet down. Why did the active feeding of a large group of whales on shallow prey over several weeks not entice these deep diving whales to join in? Segregation within a feeding ground has been observed in humpbacks, where mature individuals seem to congregate on the richer and more abundant patches of food, while immature animals are found on smaller ones. Finback whales may select the feed in the same way. It is also possible that preference among individuals for different prey species in the same area may explain a division among feeding animals.

Today, researchers are learning more about the lives of finback whales by identifying individuals. By taking photographs of blazes, chevrons, and dorsal fins, they have identified and cataloged hundreds of finback whales from New York to the Gulf of St. Lawrence. Some individuals have been observed returning to summer feeding grounds year after year. The whales in the Gulf of St. Lawrence appear to belong to a distinct feeding stock separate from the Gulf of Maine. Within the Gulf of Maine, some whales return to the same feeding area year after year. Other individuals have been observed in different areas within a feeding season, or from one summer to the next.

The first whale to be entered into the

North Atlantic Finback Whale Catalog, number 0001, was named "George Washington." First photographed at Mt. Desert Rock, Maine in 1977, "George" has usually returned to that area each summer for a few weeks or more ever since. Photo identification of finback whales is painstaking work. ID photos must include the entire right side of the animal (preferably both sides), from the blowholes to the tail stock. Photographs need to be of a high enough quality to show the subtle color patterns of the blaze and chevron, nicks on the dorsal fin, and a variety of scars. Comparison of new photographs to known whales and adding new whales to the growing catalog requires patience and perseverance. The rewards are huge as the wealth of information on the species, including their life-patterns, increases every year. Recent genetic sampling, in concert with photo identification, allows researchers to determine genetic relatedness or separation between feeding stocks, sex structure between and within feeding areas, and other valuable information about the finback whale population.

Finback whale populations have been dramatically reduced from an estimated worldwide pre-whaling population of around 600,000 to less than 75,000. Estimates for the western North Atlantic start at around 16,000 individuals. The finback whale is still on the U.S. endangered species list.

Above: The tall spout of a finback whale. Finbacks breathe 5 to 15 times between deep dives lasting 5 to 15 minutes and which can be as deep as 750 feet (230 m). Unpredictable at times, finback whales may surface a mile (1.6 km) or more away from their last known position.
Photo by Stephen Mullane

Above right: A group of finback whales surfaces close to the Mt. Desert Rock light station in the Gulf of Maine. The light station is maintained by the U.S. Coast Guard and researchers from the College of the Atlantic of Bar Harbor, Maine. The island serves as a platform for ongoing long term whale and seabird research projects.
Photo by Stephen Mullane

Right: Lunge feeding finback whales. Sources of food in the oceans are found in patches. Whales are constantly on the move in search of more productive feeding areas. Once found, the prey becomes the target of rapid and powerful feeding lunges.
Photo by François Gohier

THE MINKE WHALE

Minke whales (*Balaenoptera acutorostrata*) are found worldwide, preferring cooler temperate waters to tropical waters, and are found throughout the North Atlantic. Venturing closer to shore than the larger baleen whales, they frequent island passages and sometimes enter bays and harbors. They can be seen from the shore in Maine and throughout the Canadian Maritimes where seaside cliffs and rock outcroppings provide good elevated vantage points.

The forward portion of the jaw and head is pointed, giving rise to the name "little piked whale." When the animal surfaces, it raises the lower jaw out of the water first, before lifting the blowholes above the surface. This may explain why spouts of this species are rather inconspicuous. Minkes have a tall falcate, or sickle-shaped, dorsal fin that appears at the surface at the same time as the blowholes. Surfacing 2 to 4 times with 30 to 60 second intervals between each breath, a minke whale submerges for 2 to 6 minutes. In unprotected waters with moderate waves, minke whales are seen only briefly before going out of sight.

Female minke whales are sexually mature at four years and 24 feet (7.3 m) in length; mature males at 22 to 23 feet long (about 7 m). Mating occurs in late fall and winter and is followed by a 10 to 11 month gestation. Calves are weaned quickly, at less than six months. Minke whales attain a weight of about 10 to 11 tons (9,000 to 9,900 kg) for a large individual.

Minke whales feed upon a variety of fish, krill, and copepods. Their baleen plates grow closer together, at about $\frac{3}{16}$ of an inch (0.5 cm) apart, compared to about double that in

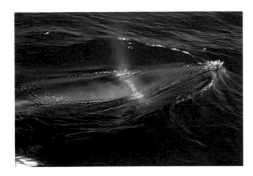

The minke whale is the most numerous baleen whale. Not hunted as aggressively as larger baleen whales, the minke whale population grew by feasting on the surplus of feed made available as blue, finback, and humpback whale populations were decimated. The minke whale has a worldwide population estimated at between 500,000 and 1,000,000. While protected under the International Whaling Commission moratorium on commercial whaling declared in 1986, minke whales are still hunted under so-called "research permits" issued by the IWC to nations such as Japan, Norway and more recently Iceland.
Photo by Beverly Agler

other baleen whales. Minkes have 270 to 350 baleen plates on each side of the mouth. The frayed baleen bristles form a mat fine enough to catch small planktonic copepods. This allows the minke to engulf prey like other rorquals and to skim-feed like a right whale. Many types of fish are taken including herring, capelin, sand lance, as well as mackerel, cod, haddock, and pollock. Studies of minke whales' stomach contents in more northern latitudes show they frequently feed on one prey species at a time. A smaller percentage of minke whales feed on more than one species during the course of the day.

Distribution of minke whales in the North Atlantic is segregated by age and sex. Larger mature animals tend to move farther north, with mature females reaching higher latitudes than males. Mature females also arrive earlier on the feeding grounds and depart sooner than mature males. Minke whales in the Gulf of Maine are mostly smaller juveniles. Mothers with calves are rarely seen in the Gulf's waters but are more common off the coast of Newfoundland and Labrador, where they move closer to shore than adult males. As local juvenile whales mature, it is thought that they move farther north, possibly to Newfoundland and Labrador. Where the majority of minke whales travel in the winter and where they calve is still unknown, but is presumed to be in warm temperate and sub-tropical waters. Some individuals are seen throughout the year, with sightings peaking from April to November, off the coast of Maine. Some individuals remain in northern

Left: Aerial view of a minke surfacing. The pointed rostrum emerges before the blowholes, pushing a small wave before the chin. The smallest of the rorqual whales, the minke reaches lengths of 24 feet (7.3 m) in the North Atlantic and over 30 feet (9.1 m) in the southern hemisphere. Erratic at the surface and shy of moving boats, minke whales are hard to follow on the open ocean. However, they occasionally investigate idle boats, surprising mariners.
Photo by Mitsuaki Imago / Minden Pictures

Right: Underwater view of a minke whale. White flipper patches and the diffuse white streaks sweeping from the belly, are characteristic.
Photo by Saul Gonor / Seapics

to 70 of them which run aft to just forward of the navel.

Minke whales breach more frequently than finback whales. They sometimes breach by leaping like a porpoise or dolphin, reentering the water head first with a minor splash. Other times they roll in mid-flight and land on their sides and backs, causing a much larger water commotion.

The minke's tendency to enter coastal areas results in occasional entanglements in fishing gear. Whales get entangled in lobster gear, gill nets, and in fish traps, or get entrapped in herring weirs found along the "downeast" coast of Maine and in the Bay of Fundy. Although not a threat to the population as a whole, it is a disturbing occurrence as well as a financial burden for the fisherman losing both gear and catch.

In the United States, they can be seen on most of the whale-watch excursions based in New England. Minke whales and several other species can be seen from the cliffs at West Quoddy Head, and from Campobello Island and Grand Manan Islands on the Canadian border.

Worldwide population estimates for minke whales are around 1,000,000, with estimates for the North Atlantic approaching 150,000. Because of their small size, minke whales avoided the attention of whalers for many years. Today, using a provision in regulations, Norway, Iceland, and Japan hunt minke whales under so-called "scientific" permits from the International Whaling Commission. Disturbingly, whale products from these scientific hunts end up in their national fish markets.

Above: A minke whale lunge feeding. Minke whales feed on a variety of prey, from planktonic copepods and krill, to schooling fish as large as mackerel.
Photo by Robin W. Baird / Seapics

Below: A single Minke arches at the surface in the Gulf of Maine. The tall sickle-shaped dorsal fin, small size, and secretive nature are indicative of a minke whale. The majority of individuals sighted in the Gulf of Maine are juveniles, with adult whales seen more frequently off the Canadian Maritimes and farther north.
Photo by Stephen Mullane

areas through the winter as far north as the winter ice.

Studies of large whale vocalizations, using U. S. Navy acoustic listening devices in the North Atlantic, suggest minke whales move in "waves." They seem to approach the West Indies from the north and northeast, then head to the continental shelf south of Cape Hatteras, and off of Bermuda from December to May. They reach Massachusetts and the Gulf of Maine in May. Further work using this technique may provide valuable information on the migratory patterns of this species and others.

Minke whales may, on occasion, approach idle or slowly moving boats and travel alongside for half an hour or more. This is an exciting event allowing a perfect view of the white flipper patches and the sweeping pigmentation rising from the belly up towards the back. Sometimes the whale rolls upside down just below the surface presenting a great opportunity to see the rorqual grooves. They have 50

THE SEI WHALE

Sei whales (*Balaenoptera borealis*) are the third largest balaenopterid rorqual after the blue and the finback. Along the East Coast, the sei will grow to about 50 feet (15.2 m) and will reach weights between 20 and 35 tons (18,000 to 31,000 kg). Streamlined and fast, they are known to make long passages of a 1,000 miles (1,609 km) in only a few days, averaging over 10 miles an hour (16 km/h).

Sei whales can be confused with small finback whales at a distance but upon closer observation a number of differences can be seen. Sei whales are uniformly dark above, without the white right jaw of the finback whale. The dorsal fin is strongly curved, or falcate, like that of a minke whale, with an angular bend along the leading edge. In comparison to a finback whale, the sei whale dorsal fin is located slightly forward on the back. When the whale surfaces the dorsal fin exits the water at the same time as the blowholes. The sei whale rises to the surface flat without arching its back and rolling at the surface like other rorquals. When diving after a series of breaths, they will sink below the surface, in contrast to the arched back and raised tail stock of a finback whale. Sei whales swim just below the surface, "ghosting" along between breaths, leaving a trail of "footprints" on the surface. These footprints are created by water being pushed to the surface by the upstroke of the flukes, dampening surface waves and leaving a flat circular zone of water 15 to 20 feet (5 to 6 m) in diameter.

They are found in all the oceans of the world, from sub-polar waters to the equator. Sighting data shows a seasonal migration from low latitude, warmer waters in winter to high latitude, cooler waters in summer in both the northern and southern hemisphere. There is a seasonal migration in the western North Atlantic from northern feeding grounds along the coast of Nova Scotia north to Labrador and Greenland, south in winter as far as Florida and possibly further. Individuals seen off Nova Scotia form a separate feeding stock from those off Labrador and Greenland. A similar migration occurs in the eastern North Atlantic from the North Sea in summer to the west coast of Africa in winter.

Sei whales feed on a wide variety of food. The bristles on their baleen plates form a fine mat for trapping copepods, as well as krill, schooling fish, and squid. They feed both by skimming for zooplankton and engulfing swarms of krill and fish. While not common along the east coast of the United States, there have been localized sightings of several individuals in the Gulf of Maine in recent years. Groups of up to 50 whales have been observed in a rather small area for a few weeks, even months

at a time, not to be seen again in subsequent feeding seasons. These gatherings of sei whales are thought to occur when concentrations of copepods continue to grow without the presence of predatory fish. These super-abundant patches of copepods also affect the distribution of right whales. Sei whales are often seen feeding in loose association with right whales, especially in Roseway Basin off Nova Scotia, and occasionally in the Bay of Fundy, two areas known for high concentrations of copepods. Observations of sei whales thought to be feeding upon copepods describe them as submerging with mouths open, rolling on their right sides, and continuing through the water for a minute or two before taking another breath.

Both sexes reach sexual maturity between six to twelve years of age. Ages of maturity declined in areas where whaling reduced the size of the population. Females reach a length of 56 feet (17 m), 5 feet longer than males, and produce a calf every two to three years. Mating occurs in winter with a ten to twelve month gestation. Calves are around 15 feet (4.6 m) in length at birth and are weaned after five to nine months. Sei whales typically travel in small groups and generally feed in deeper water than that of finback whales. Traveling further from shore, sei whales avoid contact with fishing gear and as far as is known, rarely suffer collisions with ships.

Above right: The narrow profile of a sei whale appears just under the surface. Known for traveling great distances in short periods of time, the sei whale is the fastest rorqual whale. With fine baleen bristles, sei whales skim-feed for tiny plankton, sometimes traveling just below the surface with mouth wide open; they will also rush to engulf whole schools of fish and krill.
Photo by Alisa Schulman-Jamiger / MMI

Right: A sei whale appears in the dark blue water of the Atlantic. It was heavily hunted, especially during the 60's and early 70's, as stocks of finback and blue whales had declined. From a pre-whaling population estimated at about 250,000 there are probably less than 55,000 remaining in the world, with a population of less than 2,500 individuals in the western North Atlantic.
Photo by Doug Perrine / Seapics

THE BLUE WHALE

In the world of whales and whale-watching there are many spectacular experiences: the vastness of the ocean, the abundance of life, the many fascinating creatures, and then there is the blue whale. On a scale of their own, the giant blue whale (*Balaenoptera musculus*), is the largest living animal ever to inhabit the earth. They have been measured up to 106 feet (32 m) with a weight of 180 tons (163,000 kg), with pre-whaling specimens probably growing longer and larger. Their size is staggering. The average size and weight today is around 70 feet (21 m) and 100 tons (90,000 kg). The tongue of the blue whale is the weight of an adult African elephant. The length of the intestines is no less than 1,200 feet (365 m)! The blood in a 100 foot (30 m) animal would weigh between 10,000 and 18,000 pounds (8,000 kg), with a volume of 1,200 to 2,200 gallons (4,542 to 8,327 liters). The heart, required to pump all this blood, is the size of a small automobile.

After watching many tall finback whale spouts, the observer will be struck by the sight of the first blue whale spout. The blue whales' spout rises and rises, leaving no doubt to the whale's identity off in the distance. Reaching heights up to 30 feet (9 m) it will, on a windy day, rise and spread as the whale exhales to form a cloudy mist the size of a small house. Upon surfacing, the whale arches and its long back continues to roll for several seconds, for what seems to be an eternity, before the small dorsal fin clears the water ahead of the tail stock and tail.

Blue whales are predominantly found in cold waters although they frequent temperate and tropical areas. They are known for migrating long distances from feeding grounds to winter calving areas, but winter concentrations and calving areas have yet to be discovered. Portions of populations remain to feed near the ice edge during the winter, often feeding in narrow cracks or leads in the ice. Inhabitants of coastal fishing villages of southwest Newfoundland talk of watching blue whales feeding in open areas in the ice during the winter months. A shop keeper told me that one winter she was able to sit in her shop along the harbor and watch several blue whales feed for over a week just a few yards from the ferry dock. This tendency to feed "in the ice" can lead to mass mortality. Changes in wind direction and currents may quickly close openings in the ice for many miles. The trapped whales, unable to find open water to breathe, will die, drowning beneath the ice.

The head of the blue whale is broad. The tip, or rostrum, is rounded and flat, unlike the pointed heads of finback, sei, and minke whales. The splashguard protecting the blowholes is pronounced. The skin has a lovely bluish cast and has, from the blowholes to the tail, irregular splashes of greyish-white, forming patterns unique to each individual. Scientists use these to identify and catalog individuals. The belly and sides have hints of yellow due to the layer of single celled plants, known as diatoms, that grow on the skin while the whales travel in cold waters. Whalermen used to refer to blue whales as "sulphur bottoms." The flippers are long and slender, and about one-seventh the body length.

Above: Sheer size and power is exhibited by this diving blue whale. Amazing to observe, a blue whale surfacing seems to go on forever as the long back proceeds to roll across the waves terminating in a tiny dorsal fin and massive tail flukes. **Photo by Mike Johnson / Seapics**

Left: Blue whales often feed near the surface on patches of krill. Here a blue whale has engulfed prey into its throat and begins the process of pushing water out through the baleen plates to consume the prey trapped there. Their mouth is capable of engulfing a section of water the size of an average living room or about 10 x 10 x 20 feet! **Photo by Doc White/Seapics**

their length and gaining an incredible 44,000 pounds (20,000 kg) in weight! This is accomplished by consuming, on average, nearly 200 gallons (757 liters) of high-fat content milk each day.

Blue whales are fast swimmers, reaching speeds of 20 mph (30 km/h). Blue whales feed almost exclusively on krill. When gulping prey, blue whales engulf a volume of water equal to 10' x 10' x 20' (2,000 cubic feet or 55 cubic meters). Utilizing their speed and cavernous mouths, they will eat 3% to 4% of their body weight, or 8,000 to 15,000 pounds (3,600 to 6,800 kg) of krill each day.

The size of the blue whale, unfortunately, became its biggest liability and the very threat to the survival of the species. As whaling was transformed from a hunt practiced with relatively simple weapons and small ships to an industry using fast catcher boats with cannon-fired, exploding harpoons, that towed dead whales to huge factory ships, the future of the blue whale became bleak. The sheer size of the animal and the profits generated by a single kill motivated the rapid and nearly complete destruction of the species.

New chemical processes developed in the early part of the 20th century eliminated the offensive odor from margarine made with whale oil. This increased the demand for whale products, especially in countries where dairy farming was scarce. Profits from whaling increased and the demise of the fast moving blue, finback, and sei whales began. In a few short decades, from 1910 to 1965, the estimated world population of blue whales was reduced from 300,000 to a level where only a hundred or so could be found each year. Some believed that populations were so low that blue whales would not be able to find potential mates to reproduce.

Fortunately, some pockets of blue whales have survived. The present world population is estimated at around 15,000 Individuals. A population of 2,000 off the California coast shows signs of growth. Blue whales are extremely rare in continental shelf waters along the east coast of the United States. A population of more than 300 has been documented in the Gulf of St. Lawrence. These whales are seen during the summer and fall along the northern shore of the Gulf of St. Lawrence from the mouth of the St. Lawrence and Saguenay Rivers northeast to the Strait de Belle Isle. Several whale-watching excursions and research groups along the north shore offer opportunities to view these inspiring animals.

The small dorsal fin, usually less than 1 foot high (30cm), is located three-quarters of the way back on the body compared to two-thirds for a finback or sei whale. The flukes are broad and triangular, sometimes reaching a width one-quarter the body length. The tail stock is narrow and tall like that of a finback whale.

Sexual maturity is reached between 5 and 10 years. Females produce a calf every 2 to 3 years. Calves are born after an eleven month gestation. The growth of a calf is phenomenal. Averaging around 23 feet (7 m) long and between 6,600 and nearly 9,000 pounds (3,000 to 4,000 kg) in weight at birth, calves are weaned seven months later after doubling

Above: The blue whale is the largest animal ever to have lived on the planet. The blue whale has a spout that can reach thirty feet or more on calm days. With numbers severely depleted by whaling, there are about 15,000 blue whales remaining today.
Photo by François Gohier

Right: The blue whale's body is magnificent in size and power, yet it is sleek and even graceful. In color, its upper sides are a mottled blue-grey with white to yellowish undersides. The yellowish color is due to the presence of a microscopic algae, called diatoms, attached to the skin.
Photo by Mike Johnson / Seapics

THE HUMPBACK WHALE

Although a rorqual whale like the blue, finback, minke, and sei whale, the humpback is not as streamlined as the other members of the group and has a number of distinguishing characteristics. The most conspicuous of these are the long pectoral flippers. Humpbacks average about 30 to 50 feet (9 to 15 m) in length, with large ones as long as 60 feet (18 m), but their flippers can be as long as 15 to 17 feet (4.5 to 5.10 m) for a large individual, or close to a third of their body length. When these great whales leap from the water, long flippers reeling in the air, and as they swim below the surface with a gentle up and down motion, the large flippers look like wings. The scientific name of the humpback whale is *Megaptera novaengliae*; loosely translated from Latin it means "big-winged New Englander." Humpback whales reach an average weight of 30 to 45 tons (27,000 to 40,000 kg).

The dorsal fin of the humpback whale is different from one individual to the next. They range in shape from a barely noticeable nub, to a triangle, to a long hook-shaped fin. The shape and coloration of the tail, or fluke, is important for the study of humpback populations worldwide. The underside of the flukes ranges from white to black and every variation in between. The coloration lasts the life of the animal, and the fluke's markings, scars and shape are all unique to each individual. Photographs taken of the flukes and dorsal fin allow scientists to identify individual whales within their population and groups. This "fingerprinting" method is used to determine migrations and distribution, as well as individual and population habits.

Migrating great distances between feeding grounds and breeding areas, humpback whales frequent the northeast coast of North America every summer in search of food. They delight thousands of whale watchers and tourists every year with many spectacular surface behaviors, especially breaching. Sometimes approaching boats, they seem inquisitive and usually leave the observer full of wonder, with memories and experiences that will last a lifetime. Humpback whales lift their tail flukes out of the water before a deep dive. The color pattern of the underside of the fluke is unique to each individual. The whale above is known as "Gemini" by researchers. Photographed many times over the years, Gemini is known to frequent many feeding areas within the Gulf of Maine and the Bay of Fundy and has been seen most summers for more than nineteen years. Gemini, together with thousands of whales photographed throughout the Atlantic, have provided scientists valuable information about the humpback whale population.
Photo by Stephen Mullane

Left: The head of a humpback whale at the surface. The top of the head has several rows of bumps called "stovebolts" by whalers. These bumps have highly enervated hair follicles, suggesting that they may play some role in detecting currents, or possibly prey.
Photo by François Gohier

Right: A breaching humpback whale. Observing an average of 30 to 45 tons (27,000-40,000 kg) being propelled up in the air is always an awesome spectacle! The population of humpback whales has recovered slowly since the end of commercial whaling. Protected by the International Whaling Commission, since 1963, their population worldwide totals approximately 25,000. Their pre-whaling numbers have been estimated at more than 115,000 individuals.
Photo by François Gohier

At close range, the observation of the broad and somewhat rounded head shows several rows of bumps, about the size of tennis balls, on the top of the rostrum, ahead of the blowholes and splashguard, and along the lower jaw. These tubercles, or "stovebolts" as the whalers used to call them, are overgrown hair follicles which each contain a single hair. Within the tubercle each hair is surrounded by many nerve endings, suggesting a sensitivity to vibration. These hairs may be used to sense schools of fish or krill, or detect the direction of currents. Underneath the head and mouth, deep throat grooves, typical of rorqual whales, can be seen. As the whale takes mouthfuls of water and prey, the grooves expand and then contract, allowing vast amounts of water to be filtered through the baleen.

Humpbacks are known for their acrobatics. In a typical breach, a whale brings about half of its body out of the water upright, then arches to fall back in the water on its back after a half turn with outstretched flippers. During some breaches or leaps, one will see the whale clear the water entirely or even do a bellyflop. The reason behind these amazing displays is not known. Scientific explanations vary from attempts to rid themselves of barnacles growing on their skin, to forms of sexual display, communication, or simply for pleasure.

The blow is short, about 10 feet high (3 m), and broad. Their diving sequence is also easily recognized: after each breath the whale slips just below the surface for 10 to 30 seconds, then rises again to breathe. After five or six breaths the whale begins to rise increasingly higher out of the water. After the last breath the whale tucks, then arches its body showing the dorsal fin and the shape of the familiar "hump." As the whale continues to dive, the tail stock and flukes are lifted from the water.

The life of a humpback whale is divided between feeding, migrating, and breeding. It is a never-ending cycle that has been ongoing for thousands of years. Much of their behavior, where they can be found, when, and for how long is determined by these three important activities.

Humpbacks perform one of the longest migrations of any mammal. The distance between feeding and mating grounds in parts of the world is over 5,000 miles (8,000 km). In the western North Atlantic the majority of the population migrates each year to and from breeding grounds off the Dominican Republic, south to the lesser Antilles; to feeding grounds in the Gulf of Maine, Newfoundland, Labrador, Greenland, even Iceland and Norway. Several long-term research projects in the summer feeding range determined that most whales return to the same feeding grounds year after year. Mothers bring their calves to one of the feeding grounds in the spring, and in this way each generation learns where to go for food. This behavior is so consistent that genetic differences have been noted between each of the feeding stocks.

Humpback females have a gestation period of 11 to 12 months. The newborn calf is about 13 to 15 feet (4 to 4.5 m) and weighs up to 1,500 pounds (680 kg). The calf quickly begins to nurse and is usually

weaned within a year, growing at the approximate rate of a foot and a half (40 to 45 cm) per month. Humpbacks reach sexual maturity at about 4 to 5 years. Females usually give birth about every two to three years, with some giving birth every year.

Mothers with calves linger in the warm tropical water so that the calf can grow and become strong enough to make the long journey north. The mother uses the fat stored in her blubber to produce 100 or more gallons (370 l) of fat-rich milk each day helping the calf's tremendous rate of growth of about 100 pounds (45 kg) a day! The mother can squirt the milk directly into the calves throat by constricting muscles surrounding the mammary glands. Mothers with calves are the last to reach the northern feeding grounds.

It is a busy summer for both. The mother must find enough food to replace all the fat reserves she lost while fasting in the south and while producing the fat-rich milk that has nourished her calf the past five months. The calf must learn to catch and eat solid food as well. Following its mother, it learns successful feeding techniques and the best places to hunt for food. Mothers with calves remain separate from larger groups of feeding whales. The mother must find enough food, while keeping the calf safely away from the very active feeding adults.

The calf is young and playful, and there are times when the mother is feeding deep when the calf, alone at the surface, occupies its time

by rolling onto its back and slapping the water repeatedly with its flippers. Not content with this, it may dive, lifting its tail out of the water and flipping it back and forth as if waving to the sky. A bout of lobtailing may follow as the flukes slam the surface into a froth. More boisterous breaching may follow and calves may breach time and time again until they are too tired to propel themselves out of the water. Curious calves may approach idle boats nearby. This is a wonderful time for observers; the calf may slip alongside and raise its head out of the water to inspect everyone on board. The mother may surface nearby exhaling, while making a trumpeting sound calling her calf back to her side.

Humpback whales have several unique feeding behaviors that set them apart from other whales. Humpbacks use nets made of bubbles to corral prey. A whale may dive beneath a school of fish and blow a stream of air from its blowholes in a continuous exhalation, or in short bursts. As the bubbles rise, the whale swims in a circle, or even a spiral. The rising bubbles, growing in size as they approach the surface, create a circular visual curtain, or one of sound, that concentrates the prey in its center. The whale then dives below this ball of prey to rise and charge into it, mouth open.

Seen from a boat, a ring of green water forms near the surface as the bubbles rise. As the bubbles reach the surface, fish begin to jump from the water within the circle in a last attempt to escape the rising whale. In one fluid motion the whale erupts from the depths, mouth open, amidst prey jumping everywhere, then spouts, closes its mouth, and sinks back into the water. While the bubbles surface all around, the whale takes a few more breaths and dives, repeating the scene until full or until all the prey is eaten or dispersed. Other forms of bubble nets are also used. In some areas whales will blow a long curtain of bubbles along a steep shore line, or cliff, and corral the fish between the bubbles and the shore. Other whales may use a large boat as a barrier, blowing a net a few yards out from the ship, then coming up alongside to feed. Some whales also blow giant clouds of bubbles and come to the surface engulfing fish trapped inside the effervescent water.

Groups of whales, consisting of up to twenty individuals, sometimes feed in unison. The whales dive together and coordinate their movements. Using their bodies, and maybe the flash of their long flippers, they drive a school of fish or ball of krill to the surface, where whales and fish emerge simultaneously in a mass of flesh, baleen, throat grooves, and leaping prey. After a few breaths they resume the attack, sometimes for hours, repeatedly feasting on and driving giant schools of prey for miles.

Mature males migrate to the breeding grounds early and remain there almost as long as the mothers with new calves. These males actively pursue females throughout the breeding season in hopes of finding receptive ones. Males compete with one another to secure the interest of a female and the competition can get quite rough. Short battles occur when a male, escorting a female, is challenged by one or more rival males. While jockeying for position animals bash against each other, jostling and colliding in a show of strength and maneuverability. Even though males are rarely

badly hurt, bloody cuts and abrasions on the snout and dorsal fin are common. These tests of strength and dominance provide a means for the most maneuverable and strongest individuals to pass these important traits along to the next generation.

It is here, on the breeding grounds, where male humpback whales sing their haunting songs. Adult males dive down to the bottom of a shallow tropical sea, and while upside down, suspended in the ocean, sing their song over and over, coming up for air after 20 or 30 minutes, sometimes longer. Whales sing for a few minutes, hours, or even for several days. It is thought that the singing is a form of sexual display. Observers have witnessed females investigating singing males below the surface, but how often these enticements lead to mating is not known.

The songs consist of a series of moans, whistles, and musical tones. These are arranged into patterned "phrases" and a number of phrases are combined to form a theme. Several themes, from two to nine, constitute a song. The pattern of phrases and themes is repeated in the

Left: Moving from tropical breeding grounds to polar seas each year, humpback whales travel thousands of miles each way. The grace and fluidity with which they move masks the strength and resilience required to survive violent seas while they find their way across seemingly featureless tracks of ocean, and locate the prey to sustain them.
Photo by François Gohier

Above : When the water begins to boil and turns to lighter shades of green you can be certain that a humpback whale is chasing prey below. Using a variety of bubble clouds and bubble nets, humpback whales concentrate and disorient prey just before charging through the ball of bait with mouth open.
Photo by François Gohier

Right: A pair of humpback whales in the Gulf of Maine enjoying a leisurely swim at the surface. The pectoral flippers of Atlantic humpback whales are white on the dorsal and ventral surfaces, while Pacific humpbacks are mostly black on the dorsal surface and white below.
Photo by François Gohier

same sequence, over and over throughout the breeding season. From one year to the next, the songs are modified, some themes being dropped, others changed. When the whales arrive on the breeding grounds, they start singing the previous years' song, but in a matter of weeks it is altered, and before long, all the males are singing the new song. Males singing off of the Dominican Republic sing the same song as those in the Virgin Islands, and hundreds of miles to the south off the coast of Venezuela. Amazingly, males wintering on both sides of the North Atlantic sing the same song! Humpbacks in the Pacific sing their own unique songs, while those in the Northern Hemisphere have their own unique repertoire different than those in the southern Hemisphere.

The structure, complexity, and characteristics of these songs raise many questions about their use: Why do humpbacks sing at all? Why do the songs change? Do females select mates based upon song, and what qualities lead to that selection? Do males sing in the same place year after year?

Pregnant females are the first to leave the breeding grounds. They are also the last to return the following winter. They spend the spring, summer, and fall replenishing the fat reserves needed to nourish their calf before and after birth.

Humpback whales were hunted heavily, especially in the last century. Exploding harpoons, factory ships, and swift catcher boats pursued humpback whales to the polar ice pack. By the time they were protected, 95 % of the population was gone. In spite of this tremendous loss, humpbacks seem to be making a comeback. Many studies throughout the world report encouraging news for the future of humpback whales. Several populations in both hemispheres are thought to be growing. Off Australia they are reportedly growing at an annual rate of ten percent. The western North Atlantic population seems to be growing as well, with more calves seen each year. Over 10,000 humpbacks are thought to live in the western North Atlantic, and the worldwide population is estimated at over 25,000. There are positive signs for this species, but human factors can still adversely affect their population worldwide and close monitoring programs across the oceans are needed.

THE NORTHERN RIGHT WHALE

The northern right whale (*Eubalanea glacialis*) is one of the rarest animals in the world. With slightly less than 350 individuals remaining in the western North Atlantic, it is listed as an endangered species. The sighting of a right whale is a very exciting event for any whale-watcher, first-timer or seasoned scientist.

First impressions are not always accurate, and this certainly is true for right whales. The lives and behavior of right whales offer many contrasts. They are powerful yet sensual, big and bulky, yet when compared to other great whales have the flexibility of a snake. They seem ponderous, yet possess incredible stamina and strength. They are among the largest of whales, pound per foot, but feed on some of the smallest animals in the ocean. Their survival is a poignant reminder of the consequences of our human greed, as they now swim the fine line between life and extinction. They are compelling animals that continue to inspire great curiosity, compassion, and dedication in those who have had a chance to observe them in the wild.

Seen on a calm summer's day, feeding or resting at the surface, a right whale can easily be mistaken for a barnacle-covered ledge awash in the gentle waves. The head of a right whale has numerous skin growths, or callosities, often several inches thick, which protrude from the otherwise smooth surface. These callosities form in many of the places humans have facial hair. They are found above the eyes, on the chin, and in the narrow

Hunted to the brink of extinction, a small population of northern right whales inhabits the continental shelf waters from Florida to Greenland. A major portion of the population returns each summer to the Gulf of Maine and the waters south of Nova Scotia where they feed on dense patches of tiny zooplankton. In recent years, collisions with ships and entanglements with fishing gear have caused many deaths. The typical "V" shaped blow of the northern right whale is clearly visible here.
Photo by Stephen Mullane

Left: The majestic flukes of a northern right whale rolls before a dive in the Bay of Fundy. Prized for their fine oil and baleen, northern right whales were hunted mercilessly since the 11th century when the hunt began in earnest by Basque whalers in the Bay of Biscay, off the coast of Spain and France. They were finally protected from hunting by the League of Nations in 1931.
Photo by François Gohier

Right: A courting group of northern right whales. In the Gulf of Maine, during the summer months, it is possible to see groups of right whales churning the surface of the water in a ballet of bodies, tails, and fins as males maneuver to mate with a female somewhere in the middle of the frenzy. These summer courtship groups are thought to be precursors to more successful late fall and winter breeding attempts, which would correspond with normal winter calving periods.
Photo by François Gohier

ridge running from the upper lip to the blowholes, suggestive of eyebrows, beard, and mustache. These rough callosities are grey-black in color. They are the home for several species of whale lice, or cyamid crustaceans, which make them appear pinkish, yellow, or orange. Cyamids attach themselves to the skin of the whale with hook-shaped legs and feed on the skin of the whale and on copepods, some of the right whale's prey.

The head of the right whale has a curious shape. The margins of the upper and lower lip on both sides form a high arch as it runs aft and continues downward, almost encircling the eye. While feeding, the upper portion of the lower lip supports the ends of the extremely long baleen plates and forms an exit for the water entering the mouth and flowing out through the baleen. They have up to 390 plates on each side. The right whale's feeding method does not require the long "rorqual grooves" expanding and contracting along the throat to squeeze water out of the mouth.

Right whales are black in color. The ventral surface is black with some individuals possessing irregular pure white patches on their throats and bellies. The ventral surface of the flukes is also black. Posterior to the blowholes the whale widens to an incredible girth creating a nearly flat surface for many feet behind the blowholes. Right whales lack a dorsal fin. The tail is triangular in shape and up to 19 feet wide (5.70 m) with a smooth concave trailing edge and a deep median notch. The flippers are large and almost rectangular. The whales grow to 50 feet (15 m) and can weigh up to an astonishing 100 tons (90,000 kg)!

The spout of the right whale is short and bushy. Wide-spaced blowholes create a characteristic "V" shaped spout when seen from in front or behind. The spout of mature humpbacks may look similar in shape and may be confused as a right whale until a dorsal fin, or patterned flukes are observed. The right whale usually takes from 5 to 15 breaths, 5 to 30 seconds apart and then dives. This terminal dive is usually preceded by the raising of the distinctive deeply notched flukes. Right whales stay down 20 minutes or more, and will sometimes resurface near the diving point. Massive and slow, the right whales are surprisingly fluid, flexible, and even acrobatic, and are sometimes seen breaching many times in a row.

Right whale distribution along the continental shelf waters changes throughout the year. During the winter months, mother and calf pairs and a few juveniles are found in shallow coastal waters off of northern Florida and southern Georgia. This area is considered an important nursery for the species. These pairs stay close to shore in relatively calm, warm water. They depart in March and head north. Meanwhile, there are a number of right whales seen in Cape Cod Bay, especially during the month of February. During April and May there is an increase in the number of right whales being observed in the waters of the Great South Channel and of southwestern Georges Banks. Some of these whales move north to Stellwagen Bank and Cape Cod Bay, including some of the mother and calf pairs seen in the south. By the end of May and early June the right whales leave Cape Cod Bay. They head for the

Above: The strange face of a northern right whale. The incredible girth, the cyamid encrusted callosities, and the high arching mouth line of the right whale creates a bizarre looking creature.
Photo by François Gohier

Cod, where some remain throughout the winter. A portion of the population heads south, pregnant females migrate to the coastal waters off Florida and Georgia, while the remaining population seems to vanish, only to return in the spring the following year.

In general, right whales are highly mobile, as seen by their seasonal movements. Movements within the feeding season, and from one day to the next, can be far ranging. Each year, pockets of whales are found in some areas from days to several weeks at a time, not to return in following years. These short-lived concentration periods are probably related to a super-abundance of food found by a few individuals, and possibly communicated in unknown ways to others present in the general vicinity. Actively feeding rorquals like finback, humpback, and minke whales produce feeding sounds that can be heard for many miles. Whether right whales produce characteristic feeding sounds recognized by others, or if they directly communicate information about prey concentrations is not known. But the sudden appearance of a larger concentration of right whales in areas where the day-to-day occurrence of individuals has been observed to be extremely low, suggests some level of communication.

Right whales feed on zooplankton; primarily on tiny crustaceans called copepods. These copepods grow to about the size of a grain of rice when mature. They form dense swarms in the water as they follow the phytoplankton bloom.

Right whales have long baleen plates, up to 9 feet, which are terminated by thin bristles that form a fine mat capable of collecting very small prey as the whales move through the water with their mouths open. It is interesting to note that right whales and their cousins, the bowhead whales, are the heaviest of the great whales per foot in length, yet feed upon some of smallest animals found in the ocean. Right whales can be seen feeding at the surface with mouths open exposing the top portion of the head and baleen. They have been observed making sharp turns at the surface, which suggests that they are moving in response to changing prey abundance and movement. It is not uncommon for individuals to have mud on their faces, possibly indicating that these whales were feeding at the bottom. It is also possible that they might have been rubbing their faces in the mud in order to dislodge irritating skin parasites, or merely to scratch themselves.

The development of whaling as a commercial enterprise started with the exploitation of right whales by Basque whalers in the 11th century off the coast of Spain. Right whales were prized for their fine oil and long baleen. Easily approached because of their slow speed and proximity to shore, right whales were pursued and harpooned from small boats. The tendency for the carcass to float allowed whalers to tow the whale back to shore, where it could be dismembered. In the early 1500's, as the population of right whales declined in the eastern North Atlantic, Basque whalers followed their

northern and eastern regions of the Gulf of Maine, the Bay of Fundy, and the Roseway Basin between Browns and Baccaro Banks off the coast of Nova Scotia. Most of the mother and calf pairs, sighted during winter studies off Florida and Georgia, are resighted in the Bay of Fundy between July and October. The Bay of Fundy is thought to be an important nursery area as well during this time of year.

A portion of the population, mostly immature and mature males and some females, are concentrated near Browns and Baccaro Banks. Social interaction between right whales is common in this region, with groups of whales found together at the surface exhibiting courtship behavior. Groups of two to over twenty animals form, with much jostling and rolling observed at the surface as males maneuver alongside a female. The female, meanwhile, is often upside down at the surface, preventing sexual contact, until she has to roll over for another breath. This behavior has been seen throughout the northern feeding areas and is thought to be in preparation for mating during the winter months.

Females with calves usually avoid these courtship groups and the areas where they predominantly occur. In October and November, as the prime feeding period comes to an end, some of the whales from the Bay of Fundy and off Nova Scotia begin to appear near Cape

countrymen fishing for cod far to the west and established a whaling station on the Strait de Belle Isle between Labrador and Newfoundland. They continued to hunt right whales here after European colonists landed in New England in the early 1600's.

The first colonists wrote of "whales of the finest oil and baleen," in reference to right whales seen in Cape Cod Bay. The mass exploitation of right whales began, and by 1750 New England whalers were sailing farther and farther from shore in search of the increasingly rare right whale. As right whale populations declined, whalers began to venture farther afield, hunting bowheads in the Arctic and sperm whales in the Atlantic, eventually heading around "the horn" of South America into the Pacific. By the turn of the 20th century, few right whales could be found on either side of the Atlantic. Finally, right whales were protected from hunting in 1931 by an agreement of the League of Nations which went into effect in 1935.

Sixty-nine years later, right whales are still extremely rare in the North Atlantic. Scientists believe that the present-day population is less than 350 individuals. Taking into account their reproductive rate, there may have been less than fifty individuals remaining alive in 1935! Each year only a small number of new individuals is added to the catalog.

In the past twenty years, a great deal of information has been gathered from research on right whales. Photographic identification of most of the known population, genetic sampling, oceanographic sampling, and hours of observation of surface behaviors have greatly added to our knowledge about this species.

Scientists are concerned that the remaining number of right whales does not provide enough genetic variability to allow for healthy population growth. Genetic and photographic studies have shown that a smaller than normal portion of the female population is producing newborns. Northern right whales have been found to reproduce at one third the rate of right whales found in the South Atlantic. Whether this lower productivity is due to genetic inbreeding is not yet known.

The five major areas where right whales have been found are in coastal areas where there is heavy commercial shipping traffic. In recent years a number of individuals, including calves, have been killed by collisions with large ships and propellers. At the same time, the number of whales coming in contact with fishing gear is also on the rise. Though not originally thought to be a significant danger, in the last few summers several right whales were disentangled from fishing gear that had become wrapped around flippers, tails, or lodged across the mouth. A whale

known as # 2030 spent the entire summer of '99 with three wraps of gear around its torso and around both flippers. On several occasions scientists tried to help this whale; two of the wraps were removed, but the last loop was cutting too deeply into the skin and was impossible to dislodge. During a spell of foul foggy weather the whale moved well offshore only to be found dead later off the coast of New Jersey.

It is difficult to imagine what the future holds for these wonderful whales. Their distribution and movements put them in potential conflict with ships and fishing gear, and bring them in contact with pollution from the heavily industrialized cities of the East Coast. Their habit of feeding at, or just below, the surface also puts them at risk of oil spills and the ingestion of garbage dumped at sea. This combined with lower than normal reproductive rates, suggests that urgent actions need to be taken to protect this species from possible extinction in the near future.

Above right: The wonderfully graceful fluke of a northern right whale appears in the Bay of Fundy off the coast of New Brunswick, Canada. About a third of the known population of right whales visit the Bay of Fundy each year. Females bring their calves here, where food is plentiful.
Photo by François Gohier

Right: The sight of a breaching whale is always awesome. Unpredictable in nature, a breaching whale can be hazardous to researchers and mariners venturing too close. And yes, whales have accidentally breached onto boats !
Photo by François Gohier

THE BOTTLENOSE DOLPHIN

A single bottlenose dolphin shows its familiar "smile." Although popular and well known throughout its wide range, the bottlenose dolphin is not as easy to recognize at sea as it might seem due to geographical variations in coloration, overall shape, and size. They have a prominent falcate dorsal fin, a robust body, and a distinct rounded head with a beak. The color can vary, but is usually a darker bluish-grey on the back, a lighter grey on the sides, and a whitish grey underside.
Photo by François Gohier

Left: A pod of bottlenose dolphins cruise under the surface of the Atlantic. The bottlenose dolphin is found from the Gulf of Mexico east through the Florida Keys and north all the way to the Outer Banks of North Carolina and even the coast of Virginia and the Chesapeake Bay. It may also be observed more sporadically farther north during the warmer months, all the way into the Gulf of Maine.
Photo by François Gohier

Right: The bottlenose dolphin is very acrobatic and playful. It is seen lobtailing, bow-riding, riding pressure waves of other whales, and of course breaching. A single male is seen here demonstrating his talents. To the delight of observers everywhere, bottlenose dolphins are often seen in shallow waters, along beaches, in harbors, inlets, and bays. They often investigate human presence and approach swimmers, boats, and other watercrafts. When in the presence of dolphins, the observers should be careful not to follow and harass them in any way.
Photo by Doug Perrine / Seapics

Known the world over, the bottlenose dolphin (*Tursiops truncatus*) inhabits coastal and oceanic regions from the equator to polar seas. Popularized by many movies and television shows, and on display at marine life parks and aquariums around the globe, the bottlenose dolphin has become a familiar and appealing ambassador, helping efforts to educate the public about dolphins and whales.

Bottlenose dolphins are found throughout the world in tropical, sub-tropical, and temperate waters. Along the East Coast they are found from the Gulf of Mexico east and north all the way to New England. In very broad terms, two populations occur in many areas: an inshore coastal population inhabiting bays, estuaries, and protected lagoons contrasts with an offshore population, ranging along the continental shelf, the shelf break, and deep ocean basins. The inshore dolphins are generally limited to water less than 100 feet deep (30 m). The offshore portion of the population is typically found in water 100 to 850 feet deep (30 to 250 m), with additional sightings widely scattered in the deep ocean basin.

There are a number of differences between inshore and offshore stocks. Offshore populations tend to be larger and feed at greater depths, primarily on squid. Inshore animals are smaller, live in protected shallow waters and feed on a wide variety of fish and crustaceans. Some inshore dolphins prey on fish hiding in the sandy bottoms of lagoons, while others pursue fish up muddy rivers and creeks, often chasing them out of the water up onto the bank, where the dolphins, rolling on their sides, pick them up. Sometimes they

are seen literally playing with their food, flipping bait up in the air with their flukes to grab it with their mouth in mid-air. Broad generalities are difficult because bottlenose dolphins are highly adaptable, showing many regional differences in feeding habits, hunting behavior, social organization, and life histories. Inshore dolphins tend to migrate along the coast close to shore in response to a narrow range of water temperatures. Yet there are coastal dolphins that do not migrate at all, or very little.

The differences in size between the inshore and offshore stocks (but also within these stocks) are a response to variations in water temperatures, with larger individuals found in cooler water, and the smaller individuals found in warmer areas. Those found in colder water can reach lengths of 14 feet (4.20 m), while warmer water specimens average 8 to 10 feet (2.40 to 3 m). The weight varies greatly depending on geographic location, but ranges approximately between 250 and 1,400 pounds (100 to 650 kg). Bottlenose dolphins also vary greatly in coloration, generally appearing to be bluish grey with a lighter to white underside. They all have a prominent falcate dorsal fin, pointed and slender flippers, and a thick tail stock. A fairly short beak is followed by an ever-smiling mouth.

Bottlenose dolphins are powerful swimmers. They are active and acrobatic, and are loved for it. They will breach, often clearing the water by several meters, bow-ride, body-surf, flipper-slap, and lobtail. Curious, they approach vessels at sea and people on

what they have learned during their early years. Mortality is high during this transitional stage. As males reach sexual maturity, at about 10 to 15 years of age, they separate from these groups to live on their own, or form smaller male associations of 2 to 3 animals that remain together, over many years, and sometimes within the same geographical area. These bands of males may eventually help one another to select, control, and defend receptive females for mating.

The lives of bottlenose dolphins are complex and ever-changing. Changes in food abundance and distribution affect their movements and their behavior. Calving may take place during seasons when food is most abundant, or in response to the movements of predators, like sharks. The scarcity of food may also affect the time it takes individuals to reach sexual maturity, dramatically changing the reproductive rate of the population. Overfishing of local fish stocks and entanglements in fishing gear is of growing concern for the health of this species.

shore, observing us as we watch them. They may also be seen swimming with other cetaceans and riding the pressure waves of larger whales.

Females live approximately 40 years, 5 to 15 years longer than males. Maturing at 12 to 15 years, females produce calves every 2 to 4 years with the longer frequency being more common. Calves are born after a twelve-month gestation and nurse for two years, sometimes up to 4 years, progressively adding larger amounts of fish and squid to their diet. Calves remain close to their mothers and are often in physical contact.

Mothers and calves constantly call one another and maintain vocal contact. Each bottlenose dolphin has a distinctive individual call, or whistle, allowing recognition within a group, even when they cannot see each other. Mothers develop a whistle for their calves which they will learn and begin to repeat. This may take some time and much practice, but eventually calves learn a whistle and use it throughout their lives. Signature whistles help to identify each member in a group and provide a deep level of contact between calves and mothers.

Calves remain with their mothers for several years before separating into mixed juvenile groups of males and females. This is a critical time, as they now must fend for themselves and put to use

Bottlenose dolphins live in many different coastal habitats of the East Coast, but live primarily along the southeastern coast where man-made changes are occurring rapidly. Due to the increasing number of people wishing to enjoy the warm climate and the joys of coastal living, large-scale development of shorelines, new housing developments, dredge and fill operations, increased boat traffic, and more pollution have all impacted the coastal environment. The ingestion of chemical pollutants and toxins produced by red tides, also linked to man-made pollution, has resulted in the death of hundreds of bottlenose dolphins in recent years. Bottlenose dolphins must adapt to these challenges and the increasing encroachment on their environment in order to thrive and survive, but they may not be able to do so forever.

Above left: A mother with her baby calf. After a gestation of about 12 months, a single calf is born, usually in spring or summer. It will stay close to its mother and nurse for about two years sometimes longer. A calf usually weighs about 25 lbs (11 kg) and is about 3 feet long (90cm) at birth.
Photo by Doug Perrine/Seapics

Above: A bottlenose dolphin is pushing baitfish on a mud bank to feed. Highly adaptable and intelligent, they have been observed using many different feeding techniques throughout their range. They feed on a wide variety of fishes, crustaceans, and squids.
Photo by Hiroya Minakushi/Seapics

Left: Bottlenose dolphins usually live in small groups of 3 to 15 individuals.
Photo by François Gohier

White-sided dolphins feed on squid, herring, capelin, sand lance, and hake. A dramatic increase in sand lance populations in the southern Gulf of Maine during the late seventies and early eighties may have contributed to an increase in the population of white-sided dolphins in recent years.

To the delight of many whale-watchers, white-sided dolphins are fast and acrobatic swimmers who approach vessels to ride the pressure wave at the bow. They do this with most boats, from 600-foot cruise liners to twelve-foot rubber inflatables. White-sided dolphins are frequently seen in the company of finback and humpback whales, riding on their pressure wave as well. They linger at the surface as the whales dive to the depths and rejoin them when they surface, sometimes feeding on prey brought to the surface. This is to the benefit of whale-watchers as it makes it easier to know where the baleen whales will be surfacing. The white-sided dolphins usually come to the surface to breathe about every ten to fifteen seconds, sometimes with longer dives.

While living on a remote island in the Gulf of Maine, I went fishing one night in a rowboat a few hundred yards from shore. It was a spectacular night. The gently rolling sea reflected the stars and sent them dancing across the water. Gulls flew by, heading for the island to take a rest before the next day's activities. I set to work and soon was hauling in foot-long squids, one after another. I was well on my way to filling a bucket in the bilge, when suddenly I thought I heard waves cresting and breaking just to the south. They were coming closer and closer. Then I heard the calls of shearwaters, and saw in the dim light several hundred birds flying by, some landing on the water with outstretched webbed feet. Was this the wave sound I was hearing? Seconds later a school of white-sided dolphins approached and passed by me, some only a few feet away! As I listened to the wonderful sounds, I imagined this mixed species convoy; birds above, dolphins below, slicing through air and water in search of food. After they passed I set to fishing again, or so I thought. An hour later I was still waiting, without a single squid added to my bucket!

found from Cape Cod north to Newfoundland and Labrador, and across the Atlantic to the North Sea, and as far north as the coast of Norway. Some have been seen as far south as Virginia, with scattered winter sightings north over shelf waters from the Chesapeake Bay to the southern Gulf of Maine. As water temperatures increase during summer and fall, there is a northward movement into the upper Gulf of Maine and the Canadian Maritimes.

Left: White-sided dolphins swimming just under the surface in a bow-riding ballet of colors and motion. The white sided-dolphin is found mostly in the western North Atlantic.
Photo by Stephen Mullane

Above: Fast and acrobatic, the white-sided dolphin is a very social animal, often found in pods of a hundred or more individuals, as well as with other whale species such as finback whales, humpback whales, and common dolphins.
Photo by Richard Sears

Right: A mother and calf appear just under the surface of the Gulf of Maine. The striking coloration of the white-sided dolphin, with yellow and white patches on each side of the body and tail stock, as well as a tall falcate dorsal fin, make this species easily recognizable at sea.
Photo by Stephen Mullane

THE WHITE-BEAKED DOLPHIN

The white-beaked dolphin (*Lagenorhynchus albirostris*) is a slightly more robust northern relative of the white-sided dolphin. Found in colder sub-arctic waters, the white-beaked dolphin travels farther north than any other dolphin species in the North Atlantic. They are common on the continental shelf and shelf edge from Massachusetts north to Newfoundland, the Gulf of St. Lawrence, Labrador, and across Davis Strait to Greenland in the summer. Numerous sightings off of Cape Cod in the spring and later months in the Gulf of Maine and across Georges Banks, have dwindled in the past twenty years. This change is attributed to a possible regional decline in the number of squid, a favored food of the white-beaked dolphin. In Newfoundland fishermen call these dolphins "Squidhounds."

darker brownish color, or to grey, or even to black depending on distribution. Animals living within the western end of the population's range have darker beaks.

White-beaked dolphins travel in small groups of 2 to 50 animals with large herds being reported throughout the species' summer range. Herds of 1,500 animals have been observed in the Gulf of St. Lawrence and elsewhere. Seeing such large herds traveling across the ocean is an experience the observer will never forget.

The white-beaked dolphin has been seen in the company of other cetaceans including finback whales and even killer whales. It is a fast and robust swimmer that often raises its entire body out of the water when breathing. While playing and traveling it

Their range continues farther east into the Atlantic and extends to Europe, where they are often seen, especially along the coast of Great Britain, Ireland, and farther north to Norway.

Growing to a maximum length of about 10 feet (3 m) and a weight ranging between 400 and 600 pounds (180 to 270 kg), the white-beaked dolphin lacks the distinctive white and yellow stripes of the white-sided dolphin. Two diffuse white areas on both sides of the body are characteristic, one originating forward of the dorsal fin near the blowhole, extending beyond the dorsal fin, and another behind and below the dorsal fin covering the ridge of the tail stock, and extending almost to the flukes. These white patches merge on the dorsal area of the tail stock to form a sort of saddle. The white of the belly extends forward over the top of the beak. The rest of the body, flippers, and flukes are black, or dark grey with areas of moderate flecking. The mixed patterns of grey, black, and white vary somewhat between individuals. The name of the white-beaked dolphin is slightly misleading, as the beak color can vary from white to a

Above: A breaching white-beaked dolphin shows its distinctive large and robust body. Fast and powerful, it can also be acrobatic, with breaches bringing it back to the water, usually on its back or side. The white-beaked dolphin has beautiful and subdued markings along both sides of its body. With a long whitish-to-grey stripe along the entire length of the body to the thick tail stock. Two additional white to pale grey patches are found behind the dorsal fin on the upper side of the tail stock. It sometimes can be confused at sea with the white-sided dolphin.
Photo by Richard Sears

is slightly less acrobatic than the white-sided dolphin, but it will breach, usually falling to the water onto its side or back.

Because of their elusiveness, little is known about the white-beaked dolphin's social life. As far as reproduction, gestation, and even growth rates are concerned, many questions remain, as very few groups have been found stranded, precluding post-mortem inspection and studies. As sad as they are, whale strandings offer scientists an invaluable source of information on the biology and life cycles of each species.

THE COMMON DOLPHIN

The common dolphin (*Delphinus delphis*), as its name indicates, is one of the most abundant dolphin species found in tropical, subtropical, and warm temperate waters throughout the world. Exquisite in shape and color; fast, acrobatic, and playful, the common dolphin is the quintessential dolphin.

The common dolphin is easily distinguishable by the striking criss-cross, or "hourglass," coloration adorning its flanks. Two major body stripes, one tan or yellowish forward, the other greyish-white aft, form an inverted peak, or trough of dark skin as they crisscross each other below the dorsal fin. This trough and concurrent peak of grey coloration on the sides creates the darker contrasting background of the "hourglass." The trough also resembles a saddle and has inspired another commonly used name, the "saddleback dolphin." Several other markings such as a dark stripe between the flippers and the snout, a dark circle around each eye, a white underside and belly, are all distinctive. These delicate patterns can vary among the many populations of this species.

Active and fast, they are delightful to see as they go out of their way to ride before the bow of a ship. Many animals may "collect" before the ship and await the opportunity to get a free ride. When traveling quickly they make great leaps above the surface covering several meters with ease. They will often breach high out of the water, slap the water with their flippers and behave as though trained to amaze the observer.

While at sea it is possible to observe giant herds of common dolphins as they appear over the horizon. One, two, three thousand or more may pass, all around, as far as the eye can see. As these large groups weave their way through the surface, the calm ocean becomes a shimmering vibrant tapestry of motion, color, and life.

Common dolphins live for about twenty years, with males living a year or two longer than females. Males are sexually mature at six years, females at seven. Gestation is 10 ½ months with a calf born on average every 2.6 years. One of the smaller oceanic species, common dolphins reach an average length of 7 ½ feet (2.6 m) and a weight of less than 165 pounds (75 kg).

Along the eastern seaboard of North America, they are found in the Gulf of Mexico and north, following the warm Gulf Stream. Many animals concentrate along the continental shelf edge in a broad zone inshore and offshore from the edge of Cape Hatteras to the Nova Scotia Shelf. Some seasonal movements are common, but large-scale migrations are not known. There seems to be a northern shift during summer through late fall, with some animals moving into the relatively shallow waters of Georges Banks and over the Northeast Channel east of Georges Banks. Others can be found as far north as Newfoundland during late summer. These movements are somewhat associated with seasonal increases in water temperatures and distribution of prey. Squid, mackerel, lantern fish, and butterfish are common prey species.

A number of common dolphins are inadvertently killed in fishing gear each year and the effect these losses have on the population is not known. In some areas of their range, common dolphins have been hunted extensively. A distressing number of dolphins have been killed in association with the purse-seine tuna fishery in the North Pacific. Common dolphins, along with spotted and spinner dolphins, are often associated with schools of tuna. When fishermen locate a herd of dolphins they encircle them with nets hoping to capture the tunas swimming below. The entrapped dolphins may become entangled in the netting and drown. Each year thousands of dolphins perish this way. In recent years new fishing techniques brought on by consumer and governmental pressure have reduced dolphin losses, but much work remains to be done to ensure their safety.

Above right: A common dolphin pod in a surface rush typical of the species. Common to all oceans of the world, this dolphin is frequently found in huge active schools of hundreds, sometimes thousands of individuals.
Photo by Brandon D. Cole

Right: A common dolphin shows its distinctive "hourglass" pattern present on the sides of its body. The common dolphin is a fast, energetic, and very acrobatic swimmer. It will often be seen bow-riding, lobtailing, flipper slapping, breaching and even at times somersaulting!
Photo by François Gohier

The Striped Dolphin

The striped dolphin (Stenella coeruleoalba) is a strikingly marked oceanic dolphin. It has a streamlined, yet robust body, a tall falcate dorsal fin, and a distinct crease separating the forehead and the prominent beak. The flippers are small and slender with curved tips. As its name implies, the body of this species has several distinctive stripes along its sides. The most obvious stripes are two "swooshes" of light skin originating above the eye and separating above the pectoral fins. The upper stripe rises towards the base of

Above: A striped dolphin in a low fast leap at the surface. The white body stripes adorning their sides resembles an artist's impression of a streaking dolphin and enhances the appearance of speed. These energetic dolphins are denizens of the deep ocean basin and the edge of the continental shelf. Their sighting usually hints of the presence of other whales and dolphins.
Photo by Doug Perrine / Seapics

the dorsal fin, whereas the lower stripe runs the length of the body. These lighter colored stripes contrast markedly with the dark beak, head, back, and dorsal fin. When seen swimming just below the surface, these stripes appear blue in color. In addition to these two stripes, several distinctive black stripes originate near the eye: one between the eye and the dark pectoral fin, another from the eye to the anal vent, and a third, like a drawn-out eyebrow, originates between the other two and ends above the pectoral fin. The belly of this species is a creamy white, often showing pink when they leap out of the water.

Striped dolphins are found worldwide, in tropical, subtropical, and temperate seas where the sea surface temperature is above 71.6 degrees Fahrenheit (22° Celsius). Common in the Gulf of Mexico and along the edge of the continental shelf from the Caribbean to the Mid-Atlantic states, these dolphins are also found along the southern edge of Georges Banks and in southern Nova Scotia. Striped dolphins have been seen as far north as Newfoundland in the late summer and fall, and in the deep waters of "the Gully" off of Sable Island, Nova Scotia. In the western North Atlantic, striped dolphins are found in waters over 3,000 feet (1,000 m) deep.

Striped dolphin males reach 8 ½ feet (2.6 m) in length, whereas females are slightly smaller reaching 7 feet (2.1 m). Adult males weigh around 300 pounds (146 kg), and although they are sexually mature at 9 years, they may not become sexually active for several

more years. Females reach sexual maturity at about 7 years. Mating season occurs in the summer and winter, with calves being born 12 to 13 months later. Weighing about 25 pounds at birth, calves nurse for a year and a half and remain with a nursing group for an additional year and a half before forming separate juvenile groups. Females calve every 3 to 4 years. The life span of a striped dolphin is believed to be fifty years.

Striped dolphins are quite acrobatic and are often observed breaching, somersaulting, backward somersaulting, and even tail spinning. They are fast swimmers with average speeds reaching about 10 mph (10 to 15 km/h), but with bursts faster still. They bow-ride in some parts of their range including the Atlantic and the Mediterranean, but usually shy away from vessels elsewhere. Striped dolphin dives last from 5 to 10 minutes and can reach depths of about 650 feet (200 m) when feeding.

Striped dolphins are found in groups ranging from a few individuals to a few hundred. It is not rare to witness larger gatherings of a few thousand striped dolphin. In larger schools, they are usually segregated into three groups consisting of breeding adults, non-breeding adults, and juveniles. They often mix with other species such as Atlantic white-sided dolphins, pilot whales, Risso's dolphins, common dolphins, and larger whales such as the sperm and minke whales. Their association with large schools of yellowfin tuna is also well documented. Tuna are active, fast, and always hunting but it is not clear which species benefits the most from this association.

The striped dolphin has a long snout or beak containing as many as 50 teeth in both sides of the upper and lower jaw. They feed primarily upon squid and small mid-water fish. In the Gulf of Mexico they also feed upon shrimp.

In the western North Atlantic, striped dolphins are occasionally killed in the drift net fishery and the New England ground fish trawl fishery. In the eastern North Atlantic, there has been an increasing number of striped dolphins washing up on the shores of France and Brittany as a result of entanglements in fishing gear. Strandings of striped dolphins occur along the east coast of the United States in the Gulf of Maine near Cape Cod.

Hundreds of thousands of striped dolphins were killed in the eastern Pacific in association with the yellowfin tuna fishery. These losses have declined in recent years due to new fishing techniques and net design. Japan has taken thousands of striped dolphins in its nearshore fisheries and plans to continue this practice, which may deplete the stock to critically low levels. Recent evidence shows that meat sold in Japanese fish markets as whale meat is often times actually dolphin meat. Sadly, this dolphin meat contains various man-made chemical contaminants, including heavy metals such as mercury. These contaminants are found at levels well above government health standards, and yet the meat is still being sold to the public.

Environmental threats, human consumption, and entanglements in fishing gear continue to be major impacts to striped dolphin populations worldwide. Public involvement, education, and research will influence the changes needed to protect the future of these populations.

THE SPINNER DOLPHIN

The spinner dolphins (Stenella longirostris) are famous for their spectacular acrobatic displays. Their name comes from their habit of leaping from the water while rotating along their longitudinal axis, both vertically and horizontally, twisting and spinning through the air with abandon. They have been observed to spin as many as seven

times before splashing back into the water. Other species of dolphins are able to somersault, as Bottlenose are often observed doing, but the spinner dolphin, and its cousin the Clymene dolphin are the only species able to spin along their longitudinal axis as well.

Spinner dolphins are found around the world mostly in deep tropical and subtropical waters at depths greater than 6,000 feet (1,800 m), but they are sometimes found in warm temperate waters. In the western North Atlantic, spinner dolphins are found in the Gulf of Mexico, along the edges of the continental shelf, and in the deep ocean basin north to the waters off New Jersey.

The species is highly variable, displaying a wide variation in shape, size, color, behavior, and habitat. In the western North Atlantic, little is known of this slender, sprightly dolphin. In the Pacific Ocean several different populations have been documented. Color patterns vary from the typical dark cape above, with lighter grey sides and a white belly, to grey with a white belly, to uniform grey. Calves are usually uniform grey at birth, and like spotted dolphins, change colors as they mature. Most forms have a dark eye, dark edges on the lips, and stripes from the eye to the flippers and to the tip of the beak .

Spinner dolphins are small and slender, with a long thin beak and a gently sloping forehead. They are built for speed. Adults grow to 7½ feet (2.3 m), and weigh up to 172 pounds (78 kg). They mature at about 5 feet (1.5 m). Adult females give birth to a single calf every 2 or 3 years after a gestation period of about 10 to 11 months. Newborns are about 30 inches (75 cm) in length

Above: Once thought to be a variation of the spinner dolphin, Clymene dolphins are now recognized as a distinct species.
Photo by Todd Pusser / Seapics

Right: Outrageous acrobatic leaps are characteristic of the spinner dolphin. Note the dark beak, and the light side coloration extending closer to the dorsal fin than the Clymene dolphin's shown above.
Photo by Michael S. Nolan / Seapics

and will feed on rich maternal milk for up to 14 months.

In the Pacific, spinner dolphins have a pointed triangular-shaped dorsal fin, which distinguishes them from spotted and common dolphins when they associate in mixed species groups. Adult males in the eastern Pacific have dorsal fins that curve forward along the leading edge, as well as a large ventral ridge or bump posterior to the anus. The dorsal fin of Atlantic spinner dolphins is more curved than those of Pacific spinner dolphins.

The Spinner dolphin, unlike many other dolphin species, feeds primarily at night when prey associated with the deep scattering water layer rise toward the surface. The Spinner feeds upon fish and various species of squid.

Spinner dolphins usually travel in groups of up to 30, but are often seen in larger associations of hundreds, even thousands of individuals. Together they travel fast and often demonstrate their acrobatic ability with leaps, spins, somersaults, and bow-rides. They also associate with other cetacean species as well as large schools of tuna.

In the Gulf of Mexico and throughout the Caribbean, populations of the clymene dolphin (Stenella clymene) and spinner dolphin overlap. The clymene was originally thought to be a variation of the spinner dolphin, but was classified as a separate species in 1981. The clymene dolphin is shorter, with a length of 6 ½ feet (2 m), and more robust than the spinner dolphin, with subtle differences in color pattern. The lips of the clymene dolphin are darker and a dark line from the tip of the beak to the melon is distinctive. The dark cape of the back extends lower along the sides just below the dorsal fin nearly meeting the white of the belly. The clymene was known as the short-snouted spinner dolphin, in contrast with the long-snouted spinner dolphin, now simply classified as spinner dolphin. Their distribution is not as well-documented as the spinner dolphin but they have been observed in tropical and subtropical Atlantic waters. Some have been seen as far north as the coast of New Jersey.

The spinner dolphin's association with yellowfin tuna has unfortunately impacted their survival, especially in the eastern Pacific Ocean where hundreds of thousands have died as "by-catch" of the tuna purse-seine fishery. The public demand for "Dolphin Safe" tuna has successfully reduced the incidental catch.

THE HARBOR PORPOISE

The harbor porpoise (*Phocoena phocoena*) is the only species of porpoise living along the East Coast. A member of the family Phoecinidae, the harbor porpoise is one of only six members of this family worldwide.

The harbor porpoise is the smallest of the cetaceans found along our coast, with a body reaching six feet (1.80 m) in length and a weight of only 140 pounds (63 kg) for a mature male. This porpoise lives in the cold temperate and subarctic waters of the northern hemisphere, including the west coast of the United States and the coast of Europe. Smaller animals lose a greater amount of heat per body weight due to the higher ratio of skin area to body weight. Because of its small size and year-round association with cold waters, the harbor porpoise spends most of its time searching for food, and must eat the equivalent of 10 percent of its body weight each day to stay alive. In the wild they are all business, infrequently seen at play or rest.

The harbor porpoise is common throughout the Canadian Maritimes and the Gulf of Maine. Some move south in the winter where they can be seen off the North Carolina coast and as far as northern Florida. They inhabit coastal waters, where they enter bays, harbors, and estuaries. Along the coast of eastern Maine and the Bay of Fundy, where they are numerous, it is common to see them from shore as they search for a variety of fish, mostly herring which constitutes up to 90 % of their diet. Harbor porpoises move in small groups of one to five individuals. Larger groupings of forty to fifty are occasionally observed when food is abundant, or while migrating through an area.

They can be elusive and shy, very rarely approaching boats. Unlike the Dall's porpoise of the Pacific which relishes opportunities to ride the bow wave of a boat, it is an extremely rare sighting with the harbor porpoise. They are difficult to detect at sea because of their small size and because their low triangular dorsal fin is easily hidden in a slight chop. On calm days they are more easily seen in "patches" here and there while traveling through an area. The blow of the harbor porpoise is small, and thus rarely seen, but can be heard as a soft, distinguishable "pop" or "puff," giving them the name "puffing pig", or "puffer" in certain areas.

They are often associated with humpback and finback whales when fish schools are plentiful. As with dolphins, seabirds follow groups of porpoises as the foraging toothed whales chase fish to the surface where they are easily scooped up by the hungry birds.

Females mature at 3 to 6 years of age and produce a calf each year. Gestation is around 11 months. In the Gulf of Maine, mothers with newborns are common from late spring to early summer. Harbor porpoises have a life expectancy of only 10 to 15 years.

Harbor porpoises are under increasing pressure as many are killed in a variety of fishing gear, especially herring weirs and gill nets. Their population is considered threatened. Annual loss due to incidental catches in fishing gear is as high as 4 percent. Researchers, in association with wildlife managers and fishermen, are working together to reduce the losses that threaten this species. Harbor porpoises roam widely and their movements as a species are not predictable, adding to the difficulty of managing fishing activities and limit the impact on their population.

Above left: A rare underwater image of a North Atlantic harbor porpoise.
Photo by Florian Graner / Seapics

Above: The harbor porpoise is found from Cape Hatteras, in North Carolina, to Greenland. It is frequently seen in the Gulf of Maine.
Photo by Beverly Agler

Left: The distinguishable short triangular dorsal fin of the harbor porpoise is clearly seen here. The harbor porpoise is usually quite shy of moving boats but will sometimes approach motionless crafts on calm seas.
Photo by Beverly Agler

THE SPERM WHALE

Sperm whales (*Physeter macrocephalus*) are perhaps the most easily recognized whales throughout the world because of their unique physical appearance and their wide distribution.

The sperm whale is the largest of the toothed whales: males average about 49 to 59 feet (15 to 18 m) and weigh up to 50 tons (45,000 kg). Females reach lengths of 36 to 39 feet (11 to 12 m) and average about 20 tons (18,000 kg). A bizarre looking creature indeed, it carries a huge squared and blunted head, one-quarter to one-third of the body length. The brownish to grey skin is rippled and creased. The dorsal ridge has a hump-like dorsal fin and a series of bumps running down the ridge to the tail. The narrow and long, underslung jaw looks out of place on such a large creature, while the wide powerful flukes exceed width-to-body length ratios of any other whale. Even the single blowhole is odd, positioned forward and off to the left side, it produces a low angular spout.

It is the head of the sperm whale that gathers so much attention, for not only is its size remarkable, but all its functions are still not fully understood. The head contains several, large oil-filled structures that lie on top of the skull and upper jaw bones. One structure, the "case," is filled with a fine-grade oil known as "spermaceti." This oil was highly prized by whalers around the world as a lubricant used in precision machines such as clocks, scientific instruments, and a variety of engines. Below the case is the "junk," a series of vertical tissue layers separated by alternating layers of oily tissue and layers filled with blood vessels. At the front and back of the case and the junk, there are a number of air sacs connected by a long passageway. The forward sac has a strong muscular valve that may produce sounds used in echolocation and communication. Investigators believe that sounds produced by this valve are reflected off the forward air sac back towards the skull bones, and the air sacs behind the case and the junk. The combination of bone and air sacs reflect the sound back through the case, focusing and amplifying the sound before it exits the front of the head.

Other researchers suggest the case and junk are used as a giant buoyancy apparatus allowing the whale to maintain its position at various depths. Spermaceti oil is a liquid at normal sperm whale body temperatures, but a slight cooling of two degrees turns it into a waxy solid. When a substance changes from a liquid to a solid state it becomes more dense and less buoyant. By alternating the flow of cool water or warm blood through separate structures associated with the case and the junk, sperm whales may be able to congeal or liquefy the spermaceti oil. Changing the spermaceti oil by a few degrees, between a liquid and a solid, might allow whales to maintain a range of depths in the water column. Researchers are still unsure how these structures function, but they certainly play an important role in the survival of the species, as sperm whales

habitually dive to great depths in search of prey. These dives are a remarkable feat, for they frequently exceed three, four, or even five thousand feet. One unfortunate sperm whale was found entangled in a submarine cable at 7,220 feet (2,200 m)! These impressive dives are made throughout the day and night and are punctuated by short stays at the surface to recharge the oxygen supply in their bodies. Sperm whales remain at the surface, taking a breath every 15 seconds or so. After 30 to 60 breaths, the whale dives, lifting its flukes above the surface, descending vertically into the darkness.

Submerged up to an hour or more, sperm whales must conserve their energy to prolong their dives, in order to find prey. Researchers believe that a whale chasing prey at such depths would expend more energy then it would gain by catching several hundred pound giant squids. Some suggest they must remain nearly motionless near concentrations of prey and snap them up in their powerful jaws as they swim by. Others have suggested that the white lips of the sperm whale may help to attract squid, especially if bioluminescent chemicals found in squid get smeared on the whales' lips. While countless paintings and illustrations depict sperm whales doing battle with giant squids, these struggles are the exception. The remains of large squid up to 30 feet (9 m) have been found in some stomachs, but sperm whales are more likely to consume many smaller squid. The oddly-shaped mouth is quite effective at

Above: A large sperm whale bubbles just under the surface. Not easily seen from the East Coast, the sperm whale nevertheless frequents the deeper offshore waters, where it hunts for its favorite prey, the squid.
Photo by François Gohier

catching and crushing prey. The long, narrow, lower jaw has 18 to 25 conical teeth that grow up to 8 inches (20 cm) in length. The teeth and a portion of the lower jaw fit into sockets and a recess of the upper mouth. There are teeth in the upper jaw as well, but they are usually embedded deep in the gums and are of no use in catching prey.

Sperm whales are found from equatorial waters to the polar seas. They are typically found in water over 650 feet deep (200 m), but can be seen anywhere on the high seas. Like many other whale species, distribution can be patchy. Whalers referred to areas of concentration as "grounds," and sperm whales can still be found in these ancient hunting areas. Sperm whales are sighted in the Gulf of Mexico, and along the entire continental shelf edge of North America. Like many of the other deep-diving toothed whales, sperm whales cluster near the deep canyons along the shelf edge, and inshore where these canyons run across the continental shelf. Hudson Canyon is such a place, and sperm whales searching for prey found in this deep trench have been sighted within 50 miles of New York City.

The distribution of the sperm whale population also varies with age and sex. Male sperm whales forage farther north, with older adult males travelling to within sight of the pack ice. Females with calves and juvenile whales remain in tropical and temperate waters.

Female sperm whales reach sexual maturity at about 7 to 13 years of age, or about 27 to 29 feet (8 to 9 m). The males reach their sexual

maturity at about 10 years, or about 29 to 36 feet (10 to 12 m) but are not usually active until much later, probably in their early to late 20's. They have a low reproductive rate with a 5-year reproductive cycle, including a gestation of 14 to 16 months, a lactation period of 24 months, and a 3 to 4 year calving period. Newborns are about 10 to 16 feet (3 to 4 m) long and weigh up to 1 ton (900 kg).

Being very social, sperm whales live in a variety of important groups. Mothers with calves and their relatives form a very cohesive

group that, for portions of each day, assemble at the surface to socialize and rest. Like killer and pilot whales, these maternal pods consist of reproductive females and their calves, juveniles of both sexes, and non-reproductive females. Calves remain with their mothers for several years. Nursing for the first two years of life, calves slowly add solid food to their diet, but some individuals nurse for extended periods of time, even until puberty. This extended care is an important aspect of their social organization; sometimes females of a group will share the responsibility for the care of calves.

Sperm whales are deep-diving animals and females must leave their calves at the surface while they forage thousands of feet below. In groups of females with several calves, scientists have noted the tendency for females to stagger their dives so that at least one female is near the surface at all times. In this way, the females share contact with the young and guarantee that an adult is available to defend the young against predators. Females may even nurse calves that are not their own.

As males reach sexual maturity, they leave their natal pods and form smaller, all-male groups of equal age and size. As they grow older, these groups get smaller and smaller until the very large bulls, twice the size of an adult female, lead a mostly solitary life in cooler regions closer to the poles. Adult males migrate to temperate and tropical waters to mate with receptive females. These males move from one group to the next searching for a mate, and as a result, essential genetic mixing occurs within the population.

Unlike other toothed whales, sperm whales do not produce a repertoire of whistles, chirps, and squeals, instead they produce clicks; lots of them. A sperm whale produces a single click about every two seconds.

Above left: The powerful lower jaw of the sperm whale is armed with 18 to 25 conical teeth that can grow to 8 inches (20 cm) in length. Here the front ends of two heads are seen at the surface.
Photo by Hiroya Minakushi / Seapics

Above: A rare sperm whale full breach in the North Atlantic. Growing to lengths of up to nearly 60 feet and weighing as much as 50 tons (45,000 kg) for a large male, the sperm whale is the largest of all toothed whales.
Photo by James D. Watt / Marine Mammal Images

Left: Social groups and communication are very important aspects of the sperm whale's life. Here a large male interacts with a group of females and their young.
Photo by Flip Nicklin / Minden Pictures

These clicks are thought to be a multidirectional, long-range form of echolocation and allow the whale to know where the surface is, the location of objects, and even geographic features on the ocean bottom, as well as the presence of members of the pod, predators, and prey. Streams of clicks are thought to be used in a focused beam, helping to define shapes and individual objects at shorter distances. They are used for hunting or examining an object at close range. Sperm whales also produce clicks that are arranged in a variety of patterns. These patterns have been likened to "Morse-code," with click patterns, or "codas," arranged in more complicated and changing sequences. These codas are heard more frequently as whales gather in groups and as they are observed

socializing, reinforcing the idea that codas are important as a form of communication among members of a group. The real meaning of these codas, what they represent, or even how they are used is not known, but studies are ongoing to further our understanding of their meaning and of their use. The potential that codas offer in helping scientists understand the lives of sperm whales and their environment is extraordinary.

For centuries, images of this great whale have filled the pages of books, newspapers, museums, and art stores. In natural history museums far and wide, the bones and teeth of this whale cover shelf after shelf. Natural history museums display glass-covered cases of scrimshaw artwork made from the teeth of the sperm whale, and walls are covered with whaling artifacts, diagrams, maps, logbooks, harpoons, and even replicas of whaling boats and ships. Scattered among the paintings are photographs of prominent harbors brimming with tall

ships and masts, docks piled high with barrels of whale oil. The number of sperm whales killed during the whaling era has been estimated at more than a million, and the sperm whale was without a doubt the most heavily hunted whale species.

Luckily they survived, owing to their far flung distribution across all oceans and their great numbers before the time of whaling. Today the sperm whale lives on, as their worldwide population has been estimated at about one million individuals, possibly more. Sperm whales are protected by international law and they are listed as endangered. The recovery from commercial whaling, banned in 1986, will take many years due to the very slow reproductive rate of the sperm whale. With a gestation period of about fifteen months and a nursing period lasting about two years, the calving cycle of a female is only one calf every four to five years.

Until very recently, the sperm whale was as mysterious to us as they were in the 1700's and 1800's. Today, with better research and the application of newer technologies, we know a lot more about this strange and mysterious creature of the deep, and with this knowledge comes better odds for the sperm whale's survival well into the future.

Above left: The sperm whale is a rather curious looking creature. The head is very large, making up about a third of the body length. Even the blowhole is odd: off-center on the left, it produces a blow that is low, tipped forward and to the left side. The wrinkled skin, covering about two thirds of the body, is clearly seen here as well.
Photo by François Gohier

Above right: The broad and powerful flukes of the sperm whale are lifted high before a deep dive. Dives last on average about 20 to 50 minutes and reach depths of 900 to 2,000 feet (300 to 600 m), but regularly last up to an hour or more and may reach depths of more than 7,000 feet (2,000 m)!
Photo by Doug Perrine / Seapics

Right: Reminiscent of Melville's "Moby Dick," a young white sperm whale swims in the company of its mother.
Photo by Flip Nicklin / Minden

THE PILOT WHALES

There are two species of pilot whales found along the east coast of North America: the long-finned pilot whale (*Globicephala melaena*) and the short-finned pilot whale (*Globicephala macrorynchus*). They are very similar in appearance and virtually indistinguishable at sea. The difference in pectoral fin length (flippers), as their names suggests, is not great in most individuals and does not offer conclusive evidence on the identification of the species. The number of teeth in the jaw and the shape of skull bones may be the only means to identify them with any degree of certainty.

Long-finned pilot whales are typically found in cooler northern waters, while short-finned pilot whales frequent more southerly and tropical waters. Their ranges overlap; the long-finned venture south to Cape Hatteras in the winter, and some short-finned pilot whales move north off the coast of New York during the summer.

Pilot whales can easily be distinguished from other whales. They are medium-sized, between 12 and 21 feet for adults (3.60 to 6.50 m). They are jet black or very dark grey, and have a rounded but prominent dorsal fin and a rounded, bulbous head. The bulbous forehead, or melon, is pronounced and overhangs the snout slightly in larger animals. Pilot whales are also known as "potheads" due to the bulging shape of the head. The dorsal fin is situated well forward on the back and has a long base which is more pronounced in males than in females. The distinctive dorsal fin is elongated and rounded at the tip with a concave trailing edge. The flippers are long and pointed at the tip. They are about one-fifth of body length for the long-finned and one-sixth of body length for the short-finned, again with significant variation within each species. Also present is a faint white patch of skin shaped like a "W" on the chest ahead of the flippers, a small stripe above and behind each eye, a greyish to white

cape or saddle behind the dorsal fin, and a pale to white underbelly. All these markings are weak and barely perceptible at sea. Pilot whales have a stiff appearance from the dorsal fin forward, with a long graceful back and flexible tail stock, terminated by distinctive notched flukes.

Commonly found in groups of 10 to 50, pilot whales are typically seen along the continental shelf edge where the relatively shallow shelf suddenly drops into greater depths. Their distribution is often correlated with the movement of squid, their main prey, along this shelf, into coastal waters, and within deep submerged canyons, where squids are plentiful. To reach squids, pilot whales dive regularly to depths of 100 to 200 feet (30 to 60 m) but may reach depths of 1,800 feet (550 m) or more. They also feed on mackerel, herring, capelin, and other species of fish.

Pods of pilot whales seem purposeful in their

Above: A pod of long-finned pilot whales surfaces in the Gulf of Maine. It is extremely difficult to distinguish from the short-finned pilot whale at sea. Externally, it has slightly longer pectoral fins or "flippers." Internally, the number of teeth and the shape of the skull may differentiate the two species.
Photo by Beverly Agler

Left: A pod of long-finned pilot whales in the North Atlantic. Pilot whales are not acrobatic, but young individuals have been observed breaching. They "spyhop" and lobtail frequently. Quite social, they travel in groups of 10 to 50 individuals, sometimes up to 100. They are often seen in the presence of other whales such as Risso's dolphins, white-sided dolphins, and common dolphins.
Photo by Doug Perrine/Seapics

movements at sea. They are rarely sighted breaching or bow-riding, but are seen lifting their flukes, and are frequently observed lobtail-

ing and "spyhopping." Some individuals will, on occasion, slowly approach a small boat to inspect it, possibly spyhop alongside it to take a look, then move on. Other individuals will approach and simply roll over, the "W," or anchor-shaped patch at the throat visible as they swim along upside-down a few feet below the surface.

Adult males are larger than females. Adult males and females attain lengths of 21 feet (6.5 m) and 17 feet (5.4 m) in the long-finned, and 17 feet (5.4 m) and 13 feet (4 m) in the short-finned pilot whale, respectively. The adult weight for both species averages from 1 to 3 tons (900 to 2,700 kg) with the more robust short-finned reaching as much as 4 tons (3,600 kg). At birth, long finned calves are 5 5 feet (1.75 m) long while the short-finned calves are 4.6 feet (1.4 m) long. The length of gestation is markedly different, with recent findings indicating a 12 month pregnancy for the long-finned and 16 to 17 months for the short-finned. Mothers nurse the young for nearly two years, as solid food slowly replaces milk needs. Females are sexually mature at six years, while males take significantly longer

Above: Short-finned pilot whale reaching the surface. This species seem to prefer warmer water temperatures than the long-finned pilot whale and will be found in more temperate and tropical seas. Social, they are found in slightly smaller groups than the long-finned, with numbers usually between 10 and 30, sometimes up to 60. They often associate with other toothed whales species.
Photo Doug Perrine / Seapics

Right: A mother and calf long-finned. The bulbous head of the pilot whale, giving it the name "pothead," is more pronounced in older males. Pilot whales dive to 1,800 feet (550 m) or more to find squid, their preferred food.
Photo by Robin W. Baird / Seapics

and do not mature until they are 12 to 15 years old. Estimates of their life-span range from 40 to 50 years, with females out-living males by about 10 years.

Pilot whales have an interesting social structure. Recent research on short-finned pilot whales indicates that pods are comprised of one or more reproductive females, their male and female offspring, grandmothers, aunts and uncles, and an adult male. There are fewer adult males than females and sexually mature males probably move from pod to pod to mate with females outside their genetic family. Females have four to five calves during their reproductive years with the older mothers nursing their last calves for extended periods of time. These older females may also act as nursing aunts for other calves while their mothers are absent during long feeding dives. Biologists also believe that these non-reproductive females play an important role in the pod for the extended care of related young and for passing vital information to succeeding generations. It is possible that these older females communicate where to find food when prey become scarce, or how to avoid predators and defend against attacks.

The strong social ties within pilot whale pods and the trust conveyed to the more mature leaders greatly impacts the tendency of entire groups of whales to beach themselves. Distress calls made by animals suddenly stranded in shallow water may induce pod members to swim in close to aid the beached whales, tragically becoming stranded themselves. It is also believed that areas with strong magnetic field anomalies cause mass strandings, since pilot whales may be using the Earth's magnetic field for navigation. Strandings along the eastern seaboard is a major cause of mortality for this species.

Death due to entanglement in a variety of fishing gear, is also considered a significant loss to populations. Pilot whales were heavily hunted in the North Atlantic, especially in places like Newfoundland and the Faroe Islands, and are still harvested for meat, oil, and other products in many parts of their range throughout the world. The total pilot whale populations are unknown, but they are thought to be quite common.

THE BELUGA WHALE

The beluga whale (*Delphinapterus leucas*), or white whale, resides entirely in Arctic and sub-arctic waters and is very rarely observed south of Canadian waters in the Atlantic. They have been seen

occasionally in the Gulf of Maine, around Cape Cod, and south to Long Island. Their range includes the very northern coasts of Scandinavia to arctic Greenland and Canada, the James and Hudson bays, the Gulf of St. Lawrence, the St. Lawrence River, the continental arctic waters, the Bering sea, and Asian and Russian arctic waters. Their distribution and small seasonal movements are directly related to the movements and nature of the ice.

During the summer months many populations congregate by the thousands at the mouths of large northern rivers. Some travel hundreds of miles up river. Hundreds of whales can be seen passing just a few feet away from shore in very shallow water. Why belugas visit these rivers is not known. The river water, a few degrees warmer than the nearby sea, might provide newborn calves a more hospitable environment in which to live during the

first few months of growth, allowing them to develop a thicker layer of insulating blubber. Another possible reason for these gatherings may simply be to give them an opportunity to socialize, an activity which seems very important to these whales.

Belugas are known for their unique all-white bodies. When born, young belugas are grey-brown in color. During the first few years of life this coloration slowly fades to a grey-blue, then between five to ten years of age their coloration turns to white. The trailing edges of the flippers and flukes, as well as the dorsal ridge, remain a darker, brownish tint. The white coloration of adult beluga whales changes during the course of the year. Between summers, the skin becomes dingy, almost yellow in color. While congregating at the mouths of rivers in the summer, they molt all of their skin. This process takes a few weeks and may be assisted by the change in the water salinity, as well as by rubbing on river sediments. The skin has many fine wrinkles and creases.

Beluga whales can grow to over 18 feet (5.5 m) and weigh up to 3,800 lbs (1,700 kg), although there is a wide variation in size between isolated populations. Males are somewhat larger than females. Belugas are robust in shape with small, broad flippers and powerful notched flukes. They lack a dorsal fin, which has been replaced by a dorsal ridge. Their rounded and bulbous head carries a short beak.

Regardless of their white color, belugas are not easy to observe at sea. Slow swimmers and lacking a dorsal fin, they are easily mistaken in choppy seas for whitecaps. They do not breach, but often spyhop and lift their flukes when diving or lobtailing. Their blow is small and bushy but can easily be heard up to a few hundred yards away when seas are calm.

A very social whale, the beluga is seldom seen alone and is typically found in pods of 2 to 30 animals. Belugas are known for their use of a wide variety of sounds. Clicks, trills, squeals, moos, and whistles are used extensively for communication and echolocation and are heard easily above and below the surface, earning them the name of "sea canary."

Beluga whales have a highly developed echolocation, or sonar system. The sound focusing lens, or melon, on top of the head changes shape considerably during the emission of sounds, suggesting that belugas can fine tune the sound pulses for greater accuracy. Unlike other toothed whales they are able to send and receive sound signals simultaneously, adding to their echolocation flexibility and accuracy. These abilities may be advantageous when searching

Above left: This single beluga, seen at the surface, has yellowish molting skin. Photographed in Cunningham Inlet, Somerset Island, Northwest Territories.
Photo by Fernandez & Peck

Left: A group of beluga seen swimming underwater. Belugas are rarely seen alone and are usually found in pods of 2 to 30 animals.
Photo by François Gohier

Above right: A beluga "spyhopping" among his peers. The beluga is a low swimmer that is very rarely seen breaching. Spyhopping and lobtailing are common.
Photo by Fernandez & Peck

Bottom right: Large group of adults and calves near Baffin Island. The beluga is one of the most vocal cetaceans, with sounds easily heard above and below the surface. It is nicknamed the "sea canary" for its repertoire of loud clicks, moos, trills, squeals and whistles.
Photo by Flip Nicklin / Minden Pictures

for prey in the black depths. Because their neck vertebrae are not fused, belugas are able to nod and turn their head from side to side, allowing them to look behind them as they swim. This flexibility probably enhances their echolocation abilities and helps them in the important search for openings in the ice.

Females reach sexual maturity at about 5 years, while males take somewhat longer at 8 to 10 years. Calves are born after a 14-month gestation and stay with their mother for 2 years. Weaning takes place slowly after the first year as solid food becomes a larger portion of the yearlings diet. Calves are born weighing 75 to 100 lbs (34 to 45 kg) and having a length of about 4.5 feet (1.40 m). Some whales may live up to 30 years.

Equally at home in deep and shallow waters, beluga whales are known to dive as deep as 1,800 feet (550 m) in search of food. They feed predominantly near the bottom. Bottom dwelling fish like halibut and members of the cod family are common prey. They also eat clams and worms found in the sediments where they nuzzle the mud to uncover them. Males and females may segregate during portions of the year, feeding in different areas, as males are able to dive deeper and longer, allowing them to search for different sources of food.

Belugas number between 50,000 and 70,000 worldwide. Most arctic populations of beluga whales are healthy and growing. Some, however, are at risk of over-hunting by native peoples, or by man-made changes in the marine environment, such as the damming of rivers, activities associated with mineral exploration and extraction, and ship traffic. One of the most threatened populations lives at the mouth of the St. Lawrence River in Quebec.

This small population of roughly five hundred animals is at risk from water pollution generated by the populated industrial centers of the Great Lakes region, which flows out of the lakes and eventually into the St. Lawrence River. Contaminants in the water and sediments are concentrated in the tissues of animals that live in the river, like clams and worms, or in migratory eels that pass through the river from the Great Lakes. Belugas feeding on these species accumulate substantial amounts of these contaminants in their body tissues, especially in the fatty blubber.

Tissue samples analyzed from a number of dead whales contain levels of harmful chemicals so high that their carcasses must be treated as hazardous waste. Autopsies have uncovered a list of cancers, genetic defects, and abnormalities never before seen in whales. Tragically, the contaminants are passed onto the next generation when lactating females produce milk from contaminated fat stored as blubber. In addition to new cancers and disorders found in this population, there is evidence that the reproductive rate is lower than normal. Chemical contamination damages reproductive systems in both males and females. Sadly, this St. Lawrence River population may be doomed by the activities of humans and their influence on overall water quality.

THE KILLER WHALE

There are many wonderful sights in the whale world, but without a doubt one of the most awesome is a pod of killer whales swimming in the wild. The killer whale (*Orcinus orca*) is a striking animal that evokes wonder and respect.

Named by whalers who had observed the orcas feeding on larger whales, dolphins, and seals, the killer whale is the largest of all dolphins. It can be found in all oceans of the world, including tropical and temperate waters, but the killer whale prefers cooler northern and southern polar waters where food is more abundant. Many populations are oceanic, traveling through the high seas in search of whales, dolphins, fish, and squid. They may establish smaller feeding ranges along coastlines where consistent food supplies are present.

Killer whales are visually striking and are easily recognized at sea. They have bold black and white markings. The ventral surface is mostly white from the lower jaw to just beyond the anal vent. A white elongated patch behind the eye is distinctive. Females and juvenile males have tall, 3-foot (1 m) dorsal fins, while the dorsal fin of an adult male grows to an awesome 6 feet (1.8 m). They have large all-black, broad, and rounded flippers which measure up to one-fifth the body length on an adult male. Just below and behind the dorsal fin is a grey patch of skin called the "saddle." The uniquely-shaped saddles, dorsal fin shapes, and attending scars and nicks, provide the perfect means for the identification of individual whales by scientists.

In the North Atlantic, male killer whales average 22 to 26 feet (6.7 to 8 m) and weigh around 6 tons (5,450 kg). Females are smaller, averaging 20 feet (6 m) and 3.5 tons (3,200 kg). Males reach sexual maturity at around 14 years, females a few years earlier. Gestation is thought to be 16 to 17 months with newborns averaging 7.5 feet (2.2 m) and around 380 pounds (170 kg). Newborns are weaned somewhere between one and two years of age, sometimes later.

Killer whales are not common along the East Coast and only a few sightings are made off Cape Cod, the southern Bay of Fundy, and the coast of Nova Scotia during the summer and fall. Killer whales have been seen as far south as Florida and the Gulf of Mexico, but are more frequently seen farther north and east in the North Atlantic. Their distribution is sporadic and movements are not clearly known. Sightings range from single individuals to pods of up to fifty whales. Killer whales are not quick to shy away from

humans, they may even show curiosity towards boats. They have a low wide blow. They are often noisy, and can be quite acrobatic. Orcas often spyhop, flipper slap, lobtail, and breach.

The diet of killer whales is the most diverse of all the whales. They are known to eat more than 30 different fish species as well as squids, seals, sea lions, seabirds, dolphins, sperm whales, and baleen whales, including the largest of all creatures, the blue whale. In the North Atlantic, cod, haddock, tuna, pollock, herring, and salmon are common prey. Killer whales have been seen attacking schools of bluefin tuna and have been observed surfacing with giant 500 to 700-pound tunas in their mouths. Sightings of killer whales in the Gulf of Mexico are probably associated with the spawning of tuna in these waters. The general migration of tuna along the East Coast and into the Gulf of Maine may influence the movements of killer whales. Mariners have observed killer whales in the North Atlantic attacking a variety of marine mammals, including humpback whales and minkes. Others have watched killer whales pass through groups of baleen whales without showing any signs of interest or aggression, and the baleen whales showing no signs of distress.

Because of the type of food they eat and the foraging techniques they use to catch their prey, killer whales usually stay within a close-knit family unit formed of 3 to 30 animals, called a pod. These pods consist of relatives of both sexes and may span up to four generations. They include one or more reproductive females, their offspring, post-reproductive grandmothers and great-grandmothers, and usually one adult male.

Above: A pair of killer whales seen arching in the North Atlantic. Killer whales are present in all oceans of the world, from the equator to polar seas, but prefer cooler waters. Their rare presence in the Gulf of Maine and around Stellwagen Bank off Cape Cod has been associated with the movement of large bluefin tuna on which they feed. They have been observed along the East Coast as far south as Florida and the Gulf of Mexico.
Photo by François Gohier

Left: A killer whale "spyhopping." Killer whales are quite active, agile, and acrobatic in the water. They can often be seen breaching, spyhopping, lobtailing, and wave-riding. They are fast swimmers, reaching speeds of up to 30 mph (48 km/h), allowing them to catch fast prey such as large tuna.
Photo by François Gohier

Killer whales are extremely social animals: they travel, feed, rest, and play together in tight groups. These extended family groups are essential to the health and development of newborn and young orcas. Like humans, killer whales live for 60 to 80 years, sometimes longer. These long life spans may be important to family groups for the transfer of information and survival skills to younger generations. Varied prey species require adaptations in feeding behaviors. This is achieved through advanced levels of experience, communication, and coordination between members of a group.

Much of what we know about killer whales is based upon several long-term studies of coastal populations in the Pacific Northwest. While killer whales living in other oceans are hunting for different types of food and coping with different environmental factors and thus may have evolved distinctive social habits and life histories, studies of the Northwest orca populations provide the most detailed view into the lives of these whales.

Researchers have observed two distinctive populations in coastal waters. There is a "resident" population that is found within fairly consistent ranges, or areas. These groups live in protected waters among the inshore coastal islands, sounds and passages around Vancouver Island and mainland British Columbia, and south into Puget Sound. A southern community of three pods and a northern community of twelve pods spend a considerable amount of time traveling and feeding in these protected waters with some overlap between communities. While prey species are similar, consisting mostly of salmon, these communities show slight differences in the amount of time foraging, traveling and resting.

The other distinct population is typically found in rougher seas along the open ocean coastline and offshore islands. These "transient" whales, as they are called, have smaller pods of one to six individuals. The ranges of each population overlap; transients and residents occasionally travel in the same areas. They seem indifferent to one another as they swim in close proximity without socializing. The transients spend much of their time foraging, and some time socializing, but never seem to rest. They are mostly silent and travel close to shore in and out of coves, harbors, and close to exposed rocks where seals and sea lions can be found. They remain silent to prevent their prey from hearing them, and they usually forage at high tide when seals and sea lions are not "hauled out" on shore.

Transient and resident killer whale pods have very distinctive communication patterns. Each pod uses certain sounds that are characteristic and unique to the pod. This adds another level of differentiation between pods and reinforces ties between individuals within family groups.

Above: The powerful flukes of the killer whale. Killer whales do not dive very deep with dives reaching depths of about 100 to 200 feet (30 to 60 m) and lasting around 4 to 5 minutes.
Photo Ingrid Visser / Seapics

Above right: Researchers use the grey saddle mark aft of the dorsal fin, as well as the shape of the dorsal fin, to identify and track individuals.
Photo by Ingrid Visser / Seapics

Right: A mother and calf seen hunting in the cold North Atlantic. The killer whale has a very diverse diet which includes the largest baleen whales. They are armed with powerful jaws, with a total of 40 to 56, 3-inch long (7.5 cm) teeth. Killer whales often hunt in pods, working together as a team to herd prey before feeding on them.
Photo by Amos Nachoum / Seapics

THE RISSO'S DOLPHIN

Risso's dolphins, also named grey grampus (*Grampus griseus*) are easily identified at sea by their blunt bulbous head, simi-

lar to that of a pilot whale, by their grey color, and by a head and body covered by numerous scratches and scars. Due to a lifetime of accumulated scars, older animals may even appear white from a distance, their tall dark dorsal fin contrasting with the heavily scarred body. The origin of these scars is probably the result of fights with other members of their species, or even from encounters with squid, their favored food.

Risso's dolphins are found worldwide in warm temperate and tropical waters. They favor deep waters, usually well offshore of the coast, but may be observed closer to land when a narrow continental shelf allows prey species to move closer to shore. Along the East Coast, Risso's dolphins are found year-round near the continental shelf slope and shelf edge east of the mid-Atlantic states and south of Georges Bank. As the water warms during the summer, Risso's dolphins move north as far as Newfoundland and a few may enter the southern Gulf of Maine. With the onset of winter they move south again and offshore into deep water. Risso's dolphins are common in deep canyons cutting across the continental shelf and areas with strong currents and up-wellings. They are often found in association with the northern edge of the Gulf Stream and the large warm-water eddies that split off from the powerful north-bound current. Known as warm-core rings, these columns of spinning water meander across the North Atlantic, occasionally drifting far north into cooler water, creating short-lived, but diverse and dynamic ecosystems. Risso's

Above: The name Risso's dolphin is derived from the name of Giovanni Risso, a naturalist who described the species scientifically for the first time at the beginning of the 19th century.
Photo by Flip Nicklin / Minden Pictures

Right: Easily recognized at sea, Risso's dolphins wear the accumulation of a lifetime of scars. These scars are a testament of a sometimes violent life below the surface.
Photo by Michael S. Nolan / Seapics

dolphins are seen year-round in the Gulf of Mexico all along the continental slope from Texas to Florida. Numerous sightings are made well offshore, where the mineral rich waters of the Mississippi River create a habitat rich in food.

They primarily feed on squid, but their diet also includes different species of fish. Risso's dolphins, like beaked whales, have no teeth in their upper jaw. This is a common trait among species that feed on squid. They have about 7 pairs of teeth in the lower jaw, sometimes fewer.

These dolphins are a uniform grey at birth. As they mature they darken to almost black before beginning to lighten. An anchor-shaped pattern on their throats is similar to pilot whales. The flukes, flippers, dorsal fin, and a small area around the eye remain dark, whereas their bellies are white. The flippers are long and pointed but not as long as a pilot whale. The trailing edge of the flukes is concave with a deep median notch, and the tips of the flukes are pointed and swept back. The tall falcate dorsal fin is located halfway along the body. A shallow groove or depression can be seen between the beak and the single blowhole.

While some individuals grow to 14 feet (4.3 m), 8 to 12 feet (2.4 to 3.7 m) is more common. Males are slightly larger than females. Their weight ranges between 650 and 1,100 pounds (300 to 500 kg). Calves are usually between 4 and 5 feet (1.5 m) at birth. It is not known when this species reaches sexual maturity, but it is believed to happen as they reach approximately 9 feet in length, or before their thirteenth year. Gestation is thought to be around 13 to 14 months. They are long-lived animals with a life-span estimated at between 20 and 30 years, with some individuals probably living a few more years.

Risso's dolphins, like other dolphin species, are social animals and are commonly seen in groups of 3 to 50 individuals. They are usually seen travelling side by side, sometimes in larger groups stretching in a long line. They are quite active and often breach, spyhop, wave-surf, flipper-slap, and lobtail. Risso's dolphins associate with pilot whales and other dolphins. Their presence usually indicates that other species are not far off.

The Risso's dolphin population is thought to be quite large worldwide. Because their range is usually far offshore, making them more difficult to observe, an accurate population estimate is not easy to establish. Risso's dolphin are, unfortunately, still killed for their meat and are often found in fish markets of the Far East and in Malaysia. There is an incidental net fishery death toll throughout their entire range. These threats do not seem to have put their numbers and their survival at risk.

THE BEAKED WHALES

Along the edge of the continental shelf and out into the deep ocean trenches resides a family of whales rarely seen by humans. These are the beaked whales of the family Ziphiidae. There are approximately twenty known species of beaked whales in the world and several of these are only known from a handful of strandings or from skulls found on shore. It is very likely that other species are yet to be discovered and identified. Most of these whales live hundreds of miles from any coast, shy away from ships, and dive to great depths to feed on squid and deep-water fish.

Members of the family Ziphiidae are slender, tapered whales. They vary in size from 12 feet (3.7 m) for the lesser beaked whale (Mesoplodon peruvians) of the eastern tropical Pacific, to 40 feet (12.2 m) for the Baird's beaked whale found in the North Pacific. In the western North Atlantic the northern bottlenose whale (Hyperoodon ampullatus) is the largest, reaching lengths nearing 30 feet (9 m).

Beaked whales are characterized by two grooves under the lower jaw forming a "V" with the apex forward and by a small dorsal fin, usually falcate, two thirds of the way back on the body. They have small flippers, and have flukes usually lacking a median notch. The shape of the head varies somewhat, with most having a gently-sloping forehead and a long and narrow beak. A few species have a well-developed melon similar to pilot whales and bottlenose dolphins. The true coloration of many zephiids remains a mystery, as light and sea conditions dictate how much can be observed when they are sighted. Positive identification between some species at sea is very difficult.

Males, in most species, have two teeth in the lower jaw. Most females have no teeth, although some have vestigial teeth within the gums. The lack of exposed teeth in females suggests that the teeth of beaked whales are mostly used for social interaction and displays. The location of the teeth varies from species to species. In several species the lower teeth are located at the tip of the lower jaw. Often these species have parallel scars crisscrossing the head and body, suggesting that males rake their teeth against one another, possibly while competing for females. In several species the teeth are quite large and grow from large bulges midway along the lower jaw. In the strap-toothed whale (Mesoplodon layardii), the two teeth in the lower jaw grow over the top of the upper jaw, preventing mature males from opening their jaws completely.

Because of their pelagic nature, and the fact that some of the classified species have never been seen alive, little is known about the social interaction of these whales. When observed, they are alone or in small groups of six or fewer. Some have been observed in groups of up to 40 animals. Their diet, consisting mainly of squids, requires them to dive to great depths.

In the western North Atlantic, two species of beaked whales are more commonly observed: The Blainville's beaked whale (Mesoplodon densirostris) and the northern bottlenose whale (Hyperoodon ampullatus).

The Blainville's beaked whale, or dense-beaked whale, reaches lengths of 15 to 16 feet (4.7 m) and a weight over 2,000 pounds (950 kg). It appears to be dark blue on the upper part of the body and sides with a lighter grey or white underside. The skin is marked by patches or splatters of white or pink all over the body. Well-marked scars and scratches are also present, more so in the male. With a flattened forehead, the prominent features of the head are the two arches present in the lower jaw, from which a large tooth erupts for the male. These two teeth will reach above the upper jaw in adult males and may be encrusted with barnacles. This species has been observed at the surface in small groups, but are usually seen alone or in pairs.

The northern bottlenose whale is a robust medium-sized whale, reaching lengths of 23 to 29 feet (7 to 9 m) and a weight of 9,800 to 15,000 lbs (4,300 to 6,800 kg). It has a distinctive bulbous forehead and a prominent beak. In older males the melon is pronounced, overhanging the base of the beak by several inches (5 cm). The dorsal fin is relatively small, slightly falcate and located two-thirds of the way along the back, and is darker than the rest of the body. The small beak can be seen when the whale breaks the surface before a spout. The bushy spout is 5 to 6 feet tall (1.7 m) and angles forward from the blowhole. The flukes are sometimes raised before a deep dive.

Above: A small group of northern bottlenose whales. This species is only one of several species of beaked whales found in the western North Atlantic. The prominent beak and bulbous melon is characteristic. They dive to great depths in search of squid, fish, and even invertebrates living on the ocean floor.
Photo by Flip Nicklin / Minden Pictures

Young northern bottlenose whales are a uniform chocolate brown. The belly becomes lighter with age, revealing numerous patches and blotches sweeping up along the sides and contrasting with the sides and back. Numerous scratches and scars are evident along the length of the body, particularly on adult males. The head and jaws are lighter in color than the rest of the body.

Northern bottlenose whales are found in the temperate waters of the North Atlantic northward to the edge of the Arctic pack ice. In the western North Atlantic bottlenose whales are common in an area known as "the Gully" off the east coast of Nova Scotia and further north in Davis Strait off Northern Labrador. There may be a southerly shift in winter to Georges Bank.

Northern bottlenose whales are deep divers, with dives having been recorded at over 3,200 feet (1,000 m). Recent studies show that they can remain below the surface for over an hour. They feed primarily upon squid, but they may also forage on pelagic herring and invertebrates living on the ocean floor. They are found alone or in groups of up to fifteen animals. Whaling records show that thousands were taken around the turn of the last century for animal feed and spermaceti oil. Before this hunt it was possible to observe groups of a few hundred individuals swimming together. They have been protected since 1977.

PAST & FUTURE

A petroglyph on Washington State's Olympic Peninsula symbolizes the deep reverence that humans have had for whales, large and small, over the centuries. Adorning rocks, totems, paintings, and frescoes, from the simplest carvings on seaside rocks to the most elaborate and descriptive paintings of the industrial age, art has represented our relationship with whales around the world. Unfortunately, in our modern societies, deep reverence gave way to commercial needs then greed, and within a short time resulted in the near complete destruction of entire whale populations. Today, through education and a better understanding of human impact on the environment, greed has sometimes been transformed into conservation and protection. The future of whale populations in the world is now, more than ever, dependent on the level of reverence and understanding for our natural environment.
Photo by Brandon D. Cole

Left: A northern right whale breaching in all its beauty. Commercial whaling began with the hunt for right whales in the Bay of Biscay around the 11th century. The vast profits generated by such hunts soon created a new industry. Vessels from many countries began to navigate all the oceans of the globe in search of the magnificent giants.
Photo by François Gohier

Right: First contact is established between a killer whale and a group of young children. Although controversial, the presence of marine mammals in aquaria around the world has, without a doubt, played an important role in the education of the greater public about cetaceans and the marine environment. This is especially true for those unable to experience whales in their natural environment. Exposure to live animals in well-managed facilities has increased the level of public awareness to the plight of whales worldwide as well as to the need for more protection.
Photo by Brandon D. Cole

Throughout human evolution and centuries of history, it was the ability to hunt, to fish, and to gather food that defined the ability to survive. The presence of small and large marine mammals near shores and along coastlines has always represented a bountiful source of food to nearby human inhabitants. Aboriginal and subsistence hunters the world-over have practiced whale hunting since the Stone Age. Coastal communities relied on their skills at fishing and hunting to provide necessary sources of protein and important raw materials. For many cultures, the skills acquired while fishing, and later while hunting smaller marine mammals including seals, provided the confidence needed to hunt prey such as large whales.

While no archeological evidence has been found yet to show that true whaling cultures existed along the East Coast as they did in the Pacific Northwest, it has been established that Native American cultures took advantage of the occasional hunt for small and large cetaceans and benefited from the use of larger beached whales. Reports written by early colonists describe the manner by which American Indians used light dugout canoes to approach whales near shores and strike them with harpoons tipped with wood or stone heads. Once weakened, the animals were struck with arrows and knives. Farther north, in the western and eastern Arctic, Eskimos have been hunting whales, large and small, for possibly as long as 5,000 years using harpoons made of ivory and wood. The Eskimos hunted the treacherous frigid waters from kayaks and their larger version, the umiaks.

Eventually, the limited subsistence hunting of whales turned into commercial or profit-making enterprises. The commercial hunting of whales probably began during the 11th century, with the Basques hunting right whales in the Bay of Biscay off the coast of Spain and France. Perched atop stone towers, whalers sighted the whales from shore and approached them to within a few feet using small boats powered by oar or sail. One or more tethered harpoons were thrown into the back of the whale. Struggling to free itself, the whale eventually tired enough to allow the whalers to approach and insert a long metal lance into its heart or lungs. Once dead, the floating whale was hauled back to shore to be processed.

Even though this was a perilous and somewhat primitive hunt, the Basque whalers were quite successful and quickly depleted the local whale populations. The whalers had to extend their horizon to continue their profitable practice. Learning about the presence of many whales off the coast of Newfoundland and Labrador, the whalers made the long voyage across the Atlantic and began hunting whales along the Canadian coast by 1540. Setting up shore based whaling stations for six months of the year in the Red Bay area of Labrador, the Basque whalers managed in slightly over 50 years, to kill more than 20,000 whales. During this period, the Basque economy enjoyed a healthy growth and words of the profits generated by these hunts, as well as the increasing demand for whale products across Europe, attracted other nations. As whalers developed ways to process killed whales at sea, they were able to venture out farther and longer in search of more whales. They now attached the dead whales to the side of the ship, where the blubber was cut and stripped from the carcass and then cooked in large kettles on deck. The rendered oil was stored in barrels for the journey home.

The early New England colonists were quick to recognize the potential offered by the multitude of whales present just off the coast of their new world. From Long Island to Cape Cod Bay and from about 1640 to 1710, they developed a new whaling enterprise called "along-shore" whaling. Whales were observed from shore and small vessels, shaped like oversized kayaks and manned by a crew of six, were sent to sea to hunt the whales. The harpooned whales were brought back to shore to be processed. Blubber was turned into oil, and the baleen or "whalebone" was collected. Whalebone was used for a multitude of products including umbrella ribs, corset stays, hair brushes, collar stays, skirt hoops, even carriage springs. Whale oil had become increasingly more important in the cities of Europe and Colonial America, as it was burned in lamps to light homes and streets during the years before electricity.

In 1712, a significant chapter in the history of whaling began as a captain from Nantucket named Christopher Hussey discovered the riches offered by sperm whales, and this by accident. Blown off course far into deep water by a gale, Hussey stumbled upon a sperm whale, which he quickly dispatched and towed back to shore. As the whale was being processed it was found that the oils extracted from the head of the whale were of the finest quality. From the oil named spermaceti, a superior candle wax which was smokeless, dripless, and bright-burning could also be manufactured. In the intestines of the sperm whale was found another bounty in the form of ambergris. This smelly and waxy substance was used in medicine to treat a variety of ailments, and became an important fixative in the manufac-

ture of perfumes. Ambergris was literally worth its weight in gold.

By the end of the 1720's, the success encountered by the shore-whaling enterprises was dwindling and the advent of sperm whale hunting only meant one thing: The American whalers had to look farther out to sea for their bounty. From New England and New York ports, they first traveled north to Newfoundland, the Strait of Belle Isle and Labrador and then ventured farther north to Greenland and Iceland before heading into the South Atlantic, to the coasts of Africa and South America. By the onset of the American Revolution, coastal cities such as Dartmouth, later to be called New Bedford, Nantucket, Martha's Vineyard, New Haven, Providence, Provincetown, and other communities around Cape Cod had become important whaling centers.

Whaling nations were now sending their fleets worldwide. The commercial hunt had spread to the southern hemisphere, leading whalers into the Pacific by the 1890's. From there the hunting grounds off the coast of Australia, New Zealand, and the northern Pacific were opened. With each succeeding decade, new populations of whales were found, exploited, and destroyed by the thousands.

Throughout all this time, whalers had been limited to hunting the species that were slow swimmers and buoyant after they were killed. The fast-swimming rorqual whales were too swift to be caught by men in small boats and sank soon after they died. But the invention of new technologies changed everything; whaling was entering the modern era. It was a resourceful and inventive Norwegian named Svend Foyn who successfully built a steam-driven schooner in 1863. In 1868 he also developed a cannon capable of shooting harpoons tipped with explosive heads, and swivel-mounted on the bow of a whaling ship. The combination of faster and more maneuverable catcher ships and the new weapon was efficient and deadly. Whalers could now chase the great rorqual whales that had tempted them for so many years.

Above: This image of New Bedford Harbor in Massachusetts around 1870 illustrates the immensity of the sperm whale oil exploitation. Prized for its qualities, it was used in lamps, candles, and as a fine lubricant, among many other things. The discovery of the sperm whale as a source of fine oils boosted whaling worldwide and had a huge impact on the economic and industrial development of New England.
Photo Courtesy New Bedford Whaling Museum

Left: A sperm whale is slowly cut to pieces boatside around the turn of the century. It has been estimated that over one million sperm whales were killed during the whaling era.
Photo Courtesy New Bedford Whaling Museum

Modern whaling techniques spread from the North Atlantic to all oceans of the globe. The Norwegians led the way in what became known as pelagic whaling. Expeditions were sent to Antarctica, where large populations of blue, finback, sei, humpback, and right whales were found. The factory ships were capable of hauling the largest whales directly on board, up a ramp built into the stern, where they were butchered and processed. New chemical processes allowed the oil to be turned into margarine, soaps, and even nitroglycerin for military munitions, increasing profits and the interest of other nations in pelagic factory ship whaling. The decimation was quick, brutal, and so shocking in its efficiency that calls were made for the protection of whales to the League of Nations, both by concerned scien-

tists afraid of the extinction of some species and by whalers afraid for the health of their industry.

An attempt was made in 1931, under the auspices of the League of Nations, to regulate the industry with the signing of the International Convention for the Regulation of Whaling. The International Whaling Commission (IWC) was later established in 1948 and held its first meeting in 1949. It was supposed to become a forum to regulate international whaling. Unfortunately, without any true enforcement arm, member nations continued to hunt, disregarding the regulations and quotas established by the commission. Squabbling over scientific data and findings dragged on for years, delaying the creation of whale sanctuaries and the establishment of "protected status" for species.

As attitudes changed toward the killing of whales, and with the increased participation of non-whaling governments in the IWC, tighter restrictions were implemented, quotas were reduced along with the areas where whales could be hunted, and sanctuaries were established. These efforts eventually led to a general moratorium on commercial whaling. It was adopted by the IWC in 1982 and came into effect in 1986.

While nations debated the future of an industry and the survival of species, it is estimated that between 300,000 blue whales and 650,000 finback whales were destroyed in the Antarctic alone between 1920 and 1971. During the 1930-31 season more than 30,000 blue whales perished. Some esti-

mates put the total numbers of whales killed in the Antarctic after the introduction of the first factory ship at 1.5 million!

Whales are far from being saved. Some nations continue to hunt whales and have actually increased their annual catch in recent years. Norway, which objected to the moratorium and the protected status of minke whales, resumed commercial whaling in 1993, and continues to take minke whales in the the North Atlantic. Japan has conducted whale hunts in the Antarctic since 1987 under "scientific permit whaling." The meat generated by these hunts is nevertheless sold commercially on the Japanese market. Recently, Japan has expanded its hunts in the northern Pacific and has added sperm, Bryde's, and sei whales to the list of whales being killed. The disregard of the international moratorium by these two nations is an example of actions which could jeopardize the effectiveness of the ban on commercial whaling.

Aboriginal whaling and coastal subsistence hunting continue in many countries. Aboriginal hunting is permitted under the IWC to maintain social and economic needs of native cultures. Many coastal countries continue to hunt large numbers of dolphins and porpoises for local consumption. Although not presently regulated by the IWC, reports to its scientific committee show that stocks of many dolphin and porpoise species have been severely depleted.

Above left: A Dall's porpoise died captured in a Japanese drift net set in the Bering sea. Each year hundreds of thousands of dolphins are killed in nets.
Photo by Thomas Jefferson / Seapics

Above right: Net fisheries represent a serious danger to whales. Here a humpback off the coast of Newfoundland has become tangled in a net.
Photo by B&C Alexander / Seapics

Right: The killing of minke whales throughout the world by nations such as Norway and Japan continues to this day despite the International Whaling Commission's worldwide moratorium on whaling issued in 1986. Japan is using the provision allowing a "scientific" hunt. Recently Japan has expanded its hunt to include sperm, Bryde's, and sei whales.
Photo by Mitsuaki Iwago / Minden Pictures

Today, human activities are increasingly affecting the oceans and the life of whales. Whales are impacted by collisions with ships, entanglements in fishing gear, and ingestion of marine debris and contaminants, as well as from noise pollution disrupting whale communication and echolocation. Certain fishing activities endanger whales, as some techniques use the presence of cetaceans to find targeted fish species. For example, herring fishers in the Gulf of Maine sometimes use the presence of humpback whales to find herring schools, occasionally setting their nets within yards of feeding whales. Each year hundreds of thousands of dolphins and porpoises are killed in one kind of fishing gear or another, mostly nets.

Finding solutions to the loss of whales and the damage done to fishing gear by whales requires a basic understanding of each species, fishery activities, and how they interact. Some new practices have been tried with varying degrees of success. Acoustic devices, emitting sounds designed to scare away cetaceans, have been attached to nets but with limited success. Fishing activities have been curtailed in areas when cetaceans are known to be present, and some techniques and gear have been modified or eliminated to reduce losses.

In the western North Atlantic, whale biologists, working with fishermen and government agencies, have developed techniques to assist whales entangled in fishing gear. The use of special tools to cut and dislodge gear, satellite tags to keep track of entangled whales,

and specialized training, have resulted in some whales being freed.

The contamination of the oceans with toxic chemicals, radioactive waste, garbage, and sewage is an ever-increasing threat to cetaceans. Water pollution is not only a problem of rivers, lakes, and coastal areas, it can be found everywhere in the ocean. Even whales found in remote polar regions have toxic, man-made chemicals in their tissues.

All these threats to whale populations require research, vigilance, and action. The direct involvement of the greater public through membership in environmental groups and lobbies, participation in clean-up efforts and other initiatives are vital, as politicians will not act without pressure from their constituents.

Much of the early research regarding the anatomy, physiology, life cycles, and migrations of the great whales was based on information gathered from dead whales on the decks of factory ships. Sadly, these whales had to die in order to provide the information desired. Nowadays, the life cycles of free

swimming whales are being studied through the use of photography. In the 1970's, biologists began to take photographs of a variety of whales, quickly learning that a number of characteristic "markings" on each species could be used to identify individuals. Varied skin pigmentation and acquired markings, such as scars, were found to be as unique to individual whales within species as fingerprints are to humans. This photo-identification technique is used by researchers studying different species all over the world. Photographs are maintained as catalogs of known individuals by various research groups and are then pooled into a single catalog. This collaborative effort allows investigators from many countries and continents to share their data in order to learn more about the whales than they would on their own. For example, dozens of research groups contributed to the the North Atlantic Humpback Whale Catalog, which now contains over 5,000 individuals.

Above left: The careful study of thousands of images taken in the field helps scientists in the identification and tracking of individual whales. Here Richard Sears works on the photographic identification of blue whales, part of an ongoing project in the Gulf of St. Lawrence since 1979.
Photo by Flip Nicklin / Minden Pictures

Above: Throughout the world, harpoons have slowly been replaced by scientific instruments to study the world of whales and find better ways to protect them. In this case, a suction cup time/depth recorder fired by a crossbow onto the skin of a whale off the coast of Nova Scotia will yield information on its diving habits.
Photo by Flip Nicklin / Minden Pictures

Left: Strandings of whales, here sperm whales on the coast of Oregon in 1979, are often mysterious. About 1,000 cases of cetacean strandings in the U.S. are reported every year. Human activities, including pollution, shipping, and fishing may influence these numbers. Today, rapid response teams and rehabilitation efforts are organized to help injured and sick animals.
Photo by Robert Pitman / Seapics

Whale biologists are entering a new and exciting era in the study of whales, as many new tools and equipment provide invaluable information never available before. This data is then sorted and analyzed by new computer software. Satellite tags, for example, provide information via radio signals and satellite communication. Attached by suction cups to the skin, or bolted directly to the dorsal fin of sampled whales, they provide data on day-to-day movements for several weeks to months at a time. Some tags also provide the depth of each dive and the temperature of the water. Skin samples, providing enough genetic material for molecular analysis,

are obtained using darts shot from cross bows. The genetic samples provide information on the sex of individuals and helps the study and analysis of group structure, relatedness, and distributional differences based on sex. This provides more accurate data to estimate the health of populations and their sizes. Only limited by their imagination, creativity, and budgets, whale biologists have indeed entered a new phase in the exploration of the still very mysterious world of whales.

There is nothing quite like spending some time from shore or at sea watching whales. Today, many take the opportunity to find a strategic spot on land or venture out to sea to enjoy the company of whales, if only for an instant. From land there are many places along coastlines where whales can be observed; the use of binoculars and spotting scopes is recommended. In the Canadian Maritimes and in eastern Maine there are places where several species can be seen from shore. On Cape Cod, humpbacks and dolphins can be seen from the beaches. Farther south, along the Carolinas and especially in Florida, bottlenose dolphins frequent shallow bays, estuaries, and ports for the wonderment of observers.

To go whale-watching at sea is well worth the trip. In many places, tour boats frequent areas where whales are numerous and often active, giving the opportunity to witness natural behaviors and acrobatic displays. It is helpful to contact the operators and to do a little research ahead of time to find out where to go and when are the best times. To deepen the learning experience, a ship providing a researcher or naturalist on board to answer questions is a plus.

Above: Today's whale-watching operations often provide the assistance of an on-board naturalist to educate the public.
Photo by Doug Perrine / Seapics

Above right: Humpback whales at boatside. They are seen on many trips offshore, often displaying incredible feeding behaviors and acrobatics.
Photo by François Gohier

Right: The whale-watching industry has become a major tool in the education of the public. Fleets of modern boats are carrying millions of people worldwide for the experience of a lifetime. Wherever they are offered, a trip out to sea to experience the magnificence of whales in the wild is not to be missed.
Photo by Mark Carwardine / Seapics

Whales are more active in the morning and evening and trips at these times create dramatic settings for observations and photography.

Whale-watching has become an important industry in many coastal towns around the world and an important tool in the education of millions of tourists and whale-watchers. Studies have shown that, as participants are educated and informed about the life and the biology of whales and the conservation concerns impacting whales, while having a positive experience in their company, they are more inclined to take action to help whales and to protect their environment.

Whales possess many qualities that people find compelling and meaningful. Grace of movement, complexity of social life, curiosity, gentleness, and obvious intelligence, are qualities that generate powerful feelings within us. They often evoke feelings of compassion and empathy. In the end, experiencing the world of whales helps us understand the need to care for them, to act from goodness instead of greed.

The East Coast provides many opportunities to observe and experience whales in the wild, to truly enjoy their company, and to let them offer us life changing experiences. Seize the opportunity!

QUICK FACTS

Largest whale: The blue whale grows to lengths of 106 feet (32.2m) in the southern hemisphere and up to 85 feet (26m) in the northern hemisphere, with weights reaching 200 tons!

Smallest cetacean in western North Atlantic: The harbor porpoise averages five feet in length and 140 pounds (63kg) in weight.

Deepest diving: The sperm whale reaches depths of 9,850 feet (3,000 m) and is thought to be the deepest diving mammal.

Longest dive: 2 hours and 18 minutes, sperm whale group in southwest Caribbean, registered on November 11, 1983.

Frequent deep dives: The bottlenose whale repeatedly dives several thousand feet each day, more often than sperm whales.

Fastest: The finback and sei whales have been clocked at over 19.9 mph (32 km/h). Dolphins reach 24 mph (39 km/h).

Loudest: Finback and blue whales are the animals emitting the loudest sounds on earth, recorded at up to 188 decibels. These are low frequency sounds, at around 20 Hz, below human hearing range, which are capable of traveling over thousands of miles underwater.

Longest songs: The songs of the male humpback are believed to be some of the most elaborate and complex animal sounds on the planet, lasting up to 30 minutes.

Longest tooth: The narwhal tusk reaches 10 feet (3 m) in length.

Most teeth: Long-snouted spinner dolphin (Stenella longirostris), with up to 252.

Most baleen plates: Finback whale with up to 473 plates per side. Most throat grooves for a rorqual as well, up to 100.

Longest baleen: Bowhead whale baleen reaches lengths of 12 feet (3.66m).

Rarest baleen whale: North Atlantic Right Whale, probably less than 350 individuals remaining. The species has not recovered from the massive killings brought by commercial whalers.

Most numerous baleen whale: The minke whale has a worldwide population estimated at between 500,000 to over 1,000,000.

Most numerous great whale: Sperm whale population estimated at over one million.

Longest migrations:
Gray whale: Eastern North Pacific, 6,200 miles (9,920 km) each way.
Humpback whale: Eastern South Pacific, 5,000 miles (9,280 km) each way.
Humpback whale: North Atlantic: 5,050 miles (8,080 km) each way.

General Information:

Whale Watching Etiquette:
Remember that whales and dolphins are wild animals and should not be approached without common sense. Keep your distance and give them the right of way. Follow the rules established by the National Marine Fisheries Service; check their web site. Whales are federally protected, so follow the law. Not doing so is not only a crime, but could endanger yourself and your party, as well as the whales.

What to do in case of stranded or entangled live whales or marine mammals:

Do not touch or even approach the animal without prior consultation with a member of the Stranding Network. **Southeast region:** National Marine Fisheries 305-361-4586; **Mid-Atlantic and Northeast Region:** National Marine Fisheries 508-495-2090; **Also for the Mid-Atlantic** call the National Aquarium in Baltimore 410-576-1098.

Important Web Sites:
National Aquarium: www.aqua.org
National Marine Fisheries Service: www.nmfs.noaa.gov
National Oceanic and Atmospheric Administration: www.noaa.gov
Center for Coastal Studies, Provincetown MA: www.coastalstudies.org
Canadian Department of Fisheries and Oceans: www.dfo-mpo.gc.ca
The whale watching web: www.physics.helsinki.fi/whale (Highly recommended)
Allied Whale Program/College of the Atlantic: www.coa.edu/alliedwhale/
Whale and Dolphin Conservation Society: www.wdcs.org/
Whalenet: whale.wheelock.edu/
Gulf of Maine Aquarium: octopus.gma.org/
Whale center of New England: www.whale-center.org
The Ocean Conservancy: www.oceanconservancy.org/
Woods Hole Oceanographic Institute: www.whoi.edu/home
American Cetacean Society: www.acsonline.org
Nags Head Dolphin Watch: www.dolphin-watch.com/
Virginia Marine Science: www.vims.edu/bridge/mammal. html
On origins of whales: www.neoucom.edu/DEPTS/ANAT/whaleorigins. htm
Especially for Educators and Children:
Seaworld: www.seaworld.org (Highly recommended), visit also: www.enchantedlearning.com/subjects/whales; and www.whaletimes.com (great for children).
On Whaling: www.whalingmuseum.org/
Recommended reading:
-"A Field Guide to Whales, Porpoises, and Seals-from Cape Cod to Newfoundland." By Steven K. Katona, Valerie Rough, and David T. Richardson. © 1993 by Smithsonian Institution. Smithsonian Institution Press.
-"Stellwagen Bank-A guide to the Whales, Sea Birds, and Marine Life of the Stellwagen Bank National Marine Sanctuary." By Nathalie Ward/Center for Coastal Studies. © 1995 by Center for Coastal Studies. Down East Books, 1995.

Check Elanpublishing.com for additional links and info.

Above: Is the sun setting on the world's whale populations ? The future of the cetaceans on our planet depends on education and knowledge spreading to everyone, but especially the young. Discovery and knowledge about whales can only mean a deeper sense of love for all species and hopefully further protection.
Photo by Stephen Mullane

Right: Common dolphin bow-riding.
Photo by Carolyn Gohier

Back cover: The elegant tail fluke of a northern right whale in the Bay of Fundy.
Photo by François Gohier

ACKNOWLEDGEMENTS:

I would like to express my deepest appreciation and thanks to my family and friends who have encouraged me throughout this project, in particular Ed Elvidge and Doug Dolstad, Tom Morris and the crew at Morris Yachts. Special thanks go to Bev Agler, Judy Allen, Bob Bowman, Martie Crone, Steven Katona, Catherine Elk, Richard Sears and Caren Plank for offering support, information, and suggestions on the manuscript. Also, my heartfelt gratitude goes to my parents who taught me at an early age the wonder of the world and the gift of caring for it.
Mt. Desert, Maine 2003.